Joy @ WORK

Joy @ Work

WHEN WOMEN LEAD

Presented by **JODEE CURTIS**

JILL LEHMAN | KERRIE WEINZAPFEL | MECHELLE CALLEN
GRETCHEN SCHOTT | SARAH TURNER

Publishing support provided by
Ignite Press
55 Shaw Ave. Suite 204
Clovis, CA 93612
www.IgnitePress.us

ISBN: 979-8-9888859-2-4
ISBN: 979-8-9888859-3-1 (E-book)

For bulk purchases and for booking, contact:

JoDee Curtis
jodee@purpleinkllc.com
getjoypowered.com and purpleinkllc.com

Library of Congress Control Number: 2025908983

Cover design by Usman Tariq
Edited by Elizabeth Arterberry
Interior design by Jetlaunch

FIRST EDITION

Other Books by JoDee Curtis

- *JoyPowered®: Intentionally Creating an Inspired Workspace*
- *The JoyPowered® Family* (with Denise McGonigal)
- *The JoyPowered® Team* (with Erin Brothers, Peggy Hogan, Denise McGonigal, Laura North, Susan Tinder White, and Liz Zirkelbach)
- *The JoyPowered® Organization* (with Megan Nail and Jeremy York)
- *JoyPowered® Networking: Real-Life Stories and Advice for Getting the Best from Your Connections* (with Christine Burrows)

The Authors

JoDee Curtis

Speaker, Trainer, Author

🌐 purpleinkllc.com

in linkedin.com/in/jodee-curtis-csp-shrm-scp-cpa-064a611

🌐 getjoypowered.com/joy-at-work-extras

in linkedin.com/company/purple-ink-llc/posts/?feedView=all

Jill Lehman

ACC, CPC, ELI-MP Certified Coach, Speaker, and Human Resources Consultant

Founder & CEO, Evolve HR Group

in linkedin.com/in/jilllehman

🌐 evolvehrgroup.com

Kerrie M. Weinzapfel
Writer and Speaker

in linkedin.com/in/kerrie-weinzapfel-844aba20

🌐 my52todo.com

✉ kerrieweinzapfel@gmail.com

MeChelle Callen
Author, Coach, Speaker

🌐 mechellecallen.com

in linkedin.com/in/mechellecallen

f facebook.com/mechellemcallen

📷 instagram.com/mechellecallen

Gretchen Schott

*Growth Strategist, Leadership Coach,
Keynote Speaker, Facilitator*

gretchenschott.com

linkedin.com/in/gretchenschott

instagram.com/leadingwell_inspirations

Sarah Turner

Leadership Consultant, Speaker, and Coach

luminoleadership.com

linkedin.com/in/sarahgturner

luminoleadership.com/joyful-resilience-resources

Table of Contents

Foreword

J oy at work. For many, those three words together might sound like a contradiction—or at best, a luxury reserved for the fortunate few. In a world of looming deadlines, overflowing inboxes, and shifting workplace dynamics, *joy* can feel like the first thing sacrificed in the name of productivity or professionalism.

But what if it doesn't have to be that way?

What if joy isn't an elusive reward for climbing the corporate ladder or securing a dream job—but instead, a powerful force we can cultivate, choose, and protect, no matter our role or title?

The remarkable women who contributed to *Joy@Work* believe that joy is not only possible in our careers—it's essential. They are leaders, professionals, and truth-tellers who have lived through the highs and lows of organizational life. They share their stories not from the mountaintop of perfection, but from the trenches of real life, where burnout is a real threat, and where workplace joy requires intention, courage, and often, a mindset shift.

A recurring theme throughout this book is the concept of a *you-powered* perspective. That is, claiming your own agency and giving yourself permission to create joy on your terms. Rather than waiting for an employer, manager, or policy to shift, this approach invites you to make a shift first, one from within. Joy, in this light, becomes an act of personal empowerment. It's about showing up fully, honoring your values, and recognizing that your perspective matters.

One author highlights the powerful triad of challenge, control, and commitment. These elements, rooted in the psychology of resilience, are shown to increase well-being—and yes, even joy—in the workplace. When we engage in meaningful challenges, when we feel a sense of autonomy, and when we commit to something bigger than ourselves, we tap into deeper purpose and satisfaction. This is not surface-level happiness. It's the kind of joy that sustains.

Another contributor reminds us that *joy is a choice*. It doesn't always come naturally—especially during difficult seasons or in unsupportive environments. But choosing joy is not about ignoring what's hard; it's about deciding what matters. It's about finding light that comes through the cracks and choosing gratitude over cynicism, connection over isolation, purpose over resignation.

One inspiring chapter challenges readers to discover and lean into their superpower—the unique strength or quality that sets them apart and fuels their fulfillment. Whether it's empathy, creativity, problem-solving, or humor, your superpower can be the gateway to experiencing more joy. When we lead with what makes us come alive, we not only bring more of ourselves to work—we invite others to do the same.

The power of language also takes center stage. One author explores how the simple word "*just*" can limit our identity and impact. "I'm just an HR professional." "I just manage a small team." Words shape our experience, and by dropping the "just," we step more fully into our worth. We claim our place. And that claiming—that declaration—is part of what fuels joy.

Finally, this book does not shy away from the hard truth: sometimes, joy can't be found within the walls of our current employer. Sometimes, the bravest act of all is deciding to walk away from what no longer aligns with who we are. Whether it's changing roles, switching companies, or launching something entirely new, finding joy at work may mean forging a new path. And that's not failure—that's freedom.

Reading this book is like sitting down with a circle of wise, honest, and hopeful friends. These women don't hand out prescriptions or pretend that joy is always easy. What they offer instead is possibility. And permission. They show us that joy at work is not a myth—it's a mindset. One that can be built, one choice at a time.

So, if you've ever questioned whether joy belongs in the workplace—this book is your answer. If you've ever wondered whether you have the power to shape your own experience—the stories within these pages will show you how. And if you're ready to step into a more meaningful, energizing, and joyful version of your work life—turn the page.

The journey begins now.

Introduction

Joy@Work: When Women Lead is a compelling anthology authored by six entrepreneurial women leaders. This book is not just a guide; it is a vibrant tapestry woven from the experiences, wisdom, and insights of women who have carved their own paths in the world of leadership. While it offers valuable perspectives for men seeking to better understand women in the workplace, its primary audiences are women leaders and aspiring women leaders who are ready to embrace their unique strengths and transform their professional journeys.

The chapters chart a path to finding one's superpowers to become a more impactful leader and discovering joy in work. One of the key insights of this book is the importance of eliminating the word "just" from our vocabulary. Women often undermine their leadership abilities by thinking of themselves as lesser leaders, but this book challenges that notion, urging women to recognize and harness their resilience.

Joy@Work: When Women Lead empowers readers to reclaim their career journeys, offering tools to be "you-powered." It emphasizes the significance of having a supportive tribe but ultimately reminds us that the primary ingredient in career success is self-validation and proactive career mapping.

Through inspiring stories of resilience and individuals embracing their *challenge* mindset, applying higher levels of *control*, and remaining committed to creating value, readers will find constant motivation to grow their *hardiness* and share its untapped value with others.

The book also addresses the nature of career endings, both joyful and challenging. It acknowledges that while some endings result from planned goals and transitions, others are unforeseen. Yet, with careful planning and adaptability, women can navigate these endings with grace and resilience.

This anthology is a testament to the power of women's leadership and a call to action for women to lead with joy, love, resilience, and unwavering confidence.

Joy@Work: When Women Lead encourages readers to choose to lead with love and create joy at work for themselves and others. Leadership cannot be effectively practiced until one understands oneself. Creating joy at work requires a deep understanding of what joy means to each individual.

CHAPTER 1

Superpowers!

Jo Dee Curtis

Speaker, Trainer, Author

🌐 purpleinkllc.com

in linkedin.com/in/jodee-curtis-csp-shrm-scp-cpa-064a611

🌐 getjoypowered.com/joy-at-work-extras

in linkedin.com/company/purple-ink-llc/posts/?feedView=all

JoDee Curtis is the founder of Purple Ink, an HR consulting and talent development firm. She has a passion for helping organizations and individuals discover their talents, do more of what they do well, and find joy in their work.

JoDee brings a unique combination of prior experience as a CPA, CFO, and vice president of HR. Although she has 30+ years in HR, she is especially passionate about training and speaking to inspire others. This is evident through her creation of the JoyPowered® philosophy, which has resulted in the JoyPowered® book series and popular JoyPowered® Workspace Podcast.

JoDee speaks and trains on a variety of topics, including any of her JoyPowered® books, creativity, hardiness, and other leadership topics. Her audiences include the Society of Human Resources Management (SHRM), Indiana Credit Union League, accounting firms, and other associations and clients who come from a wide range of industries.

Always striving for personal growth, JoDee has obtained numerous certifications. These include becoming a SHRM Senior Certified Professional, a Gallup-certified Strengths Coach, a CPA, and a Certified Speaking Professional.

WHAT IS YOUR SUPERPOWER?

I suspect many of you are already thinking, *I don't have superpowers. I can't fly. I don't have a bionic eye or the power to move objects without touching them.* Yet it is easy to look at others and think, *I wish I could be that calm. I wish I could be that direct. I wish I could communicate that well.* We see those superpowers in others, but don't recognize that we possess them as well. I guarantee you that others are looking at you and thinking something similar about your superpowers. Call them what you want – gifts from God, strengths, genius – I view them as superpowers!

HOW DO YOU DETERMINE YOUR SUPERPOWER?

1. **Ask yourself these questions:**
    *   What do I do best?
    *   What was my best day at work?

    Meaning, what did I do on that day when things were rocking, when I was cranking out work, when partnerships were working well? When did I receive positive "feed-forward" comments about what I did well? When did I say (or could have said) out loud, "I love my work!" "I love my team!" or "I love my clients!" A time you called someone to tell them about your wonderful day. Bottom line, a time you celebrated!

    Well, okay, maybe you didn't do or say all of those on the same day, but you felt empowered, engaged, and full of joy. . . and excited about doing it again tomorrow!

2. **Ask others – your boss, your spouse, your peers, and those who report to you – these questions:**

   • What do they consistently see in you?

   • What do they appreciate most about you?

   • What would they want to model that they see in you?

   Be as specific as possible when asking questions. That is, if you ask very general questions like, "What do I do best?" you might get more generic responses than you would if you asked questions like, "What did you appreciate about working with me **today**?" "Why do you think we worked so well together on **this** project?" or "What positive attributes do I consistently display when we work together?" Of course, you can ask these kinds of questions about personal or volunteer relationships as well.

   > Note: If you take the approach in steps one and two, the key is to not just identify **what** you were doing, but why it was the "best of you." Maybe you solved a problem, or analyzed the numbers to figure something out, or checked something off of your to-do list. Achieving that deeper understanding is all about asking yourself questions. Did I achieve something significant? Were my instructions or requests especially coherent? Was I interacting with many people – or on my own? More importantly, can I do that more often? Can I do it again tomorrow?

3. **Take the CliftonStrengths® assessment.** This is the simplest way to discover your superpowers. Go to gallup.com/shop and take the assessment. The report (depending on which one you choose) will define your top five signature themes or all 34 of them. Follow the instructions to discover what they mean for you specifically. It is important to know that, technically, these are not yet your "strengths" until you can "claim" them as yours – that is, when you can identify how these themes have helped you succeed in the past.

When we understand the power of our strengths, then we can aim to use them more intentionally going forward. When you have determined your full 34 and know your dominant domain – the domain in which the majority of your top 10 to 12 themes fall – then you can truly appreciate and recognize your superpowers in executing, influencing, relationship building, or strategic thinking domains. We can *all* execute, influence, build relationships, and think strategically, but what is your default? Where do your true powers lie? When you understand that, then you can use those powers for good.

As an example, my superpower is influencing. I now know that I can effectively utilize my top 10 strengths, which include the influencing themes of maximizer, "woo," self-assurance, and communication (refer to my book link to find out more). I use these strengths every day as an author, speaker, trainer, business owner, developer of people and business, and as a volunteer.

> Once we have identified our superpowers, we can focus, we can be better leaders, better team and family members, more productive, more energized, and move mountains!

4. **An alternative assessment is Patrick Lencioni's Working Genius.** It is a simpler model than CliftonStrengths®, that assigns only six different traits. Two are your geniuses, two are your competencies, and two are your frustrations. I have the geniuses of invention and galvanizing, the competencies of tenacity and discernment, and the frustrations of wonder and enablement. My goal, then, is to work in the areas of my genius, but to understand

that I need a team of people around me who, at a minimum, have the genius of wonder and enablement (my frustrations). All six types are important, if not crucial, as they are the six fundamental activities of work and how things get done!

As with CliftonStrengths®, we must work as much as possible in our areas of strength or genius while being aware of the powers we don't have and still need in order to get things done.

Once we have identified our superpowers, we can focus, we can be better leaders, better team and family members, more productive, more energized, and move mountains!

LEARN FROM THE SUPERPOWERS OF OTHERS!

Look to those around you or think about others you have observed, worked with, or volunteered with. What are their superpowers? It's easy to be envious of them and think, *I wish I could do what they do* or *I wish I had their strengths, gifts, or style.* Instead, how about thinking, *what can I learn from them?*

I am very fortunate to have worked with many outstanding leaders, and, many times, I have had those envious thoughts, but I came to appreciate who I am and what my superpowers are. That being said, I also adopted some of their behaviors as my own. Of course, that didn't mean that **their** superpowers became mine, but I learned behaviors or communication styles that I admired in them.

ROXY

I started my career in public accounting working for a female partner, Roxy.

I didn't realize until much later in my career how much of an impact she had on me and my career. She was well-known throughout the firm, by our clients, and in the community as a strong leader, a volunteer – both in our profession and in the community – a technical expert, and a strong rainmaker. She was confident, strong in her faith, a great mom, and so much more. Roxy was someone I looked up to and always thought: *She has it all: a beautiful young family, an executive partner role at a prestigious CPA firm, a strong faith, and a reputation as an outstanding volunteer in the community and in the CPA profession.*

Almost 40 years later, I still remember my first annual review with her. A manager had noted in my review that I was confident and, overall, exceeding expectations in my role. I felt good about my work, but anything but confident at that time. I remember expressing my surprise to Roxy about this comment. She reinforced it, though, and gave me specific examples of how she had observed it. If you know me now, you aren't surprised, but at that time, age 21, I considered myself to be shy in the workplace. Like most new college graduates, I was figuring it out, finding my place, still unsure about my abilities and professional self.

After leaving this exceptionally long conversation with Roxy, I walked out of that room feeling two feet taller, more confident than ever before. Roxy encouraged me to not label myself as shy because she felt it could become a self-fulfilling prophecy, but to embrace the label of "confident" that she and the manager had given me. It was that choice of words that made such a difference for me.

About three years into my career, Roxy told me she served the Indiana CPA Society on a committee to encourage high school and college students to consider accounting as a career. She was looking to roll off that committee for a different one, and she had recommended me to take her position. I almost fell out of my chair thinking that I, a young professional, could take her place in any capacity! Once again, she showed her confidence in me. I excelled in that role, which, of course, increased my confidence even more! There were many more situations in which Roxy's impact on me was apparent over the next 15 years. Both direct comments and personal observations made me aware of this.

Roxy instilled in me an unwavering belief that I could achieve it all – excel in a thriving career, nurture a strong family, uphold my faith, and actively contribute to my community and profession. She epitomized the ideal role model, and her career path mirrored the aspirations I held for my own. I was privileged to witness her dynamic interactions with her husband, children, clients, and vendors.

In my eyes, Roxy possessed extraordinary superpowers: masterfully juggling numerous responsibilities, prioritizing with precision, maintaining relentless focus, and nurturing the growth of others.

MY MOM

When my dad was president of the local Lions Club, they sought innovative ideas to raise funds for the community. My mom proposed hosting a "Laugh-In" fundraiser, inspired by the popular TV show at the time that was known for its eclectic mix of music, dancing, and storytelling. She took charge of the entire production: she rewrote lyrics to well-known songs, choreographed the dances, penned the script for the emcee, and most importantly, enlisted participants to perform. She convinced my dad, the local bank president, to dance as a ballet performer, the school superintendent to serve as the emcee, and persuaded numerous local business leaders to step far outside their comfort zones.

My mom had an extraordinary gift for connecting with people and rallying them together for a noble cause. Her goal was to help them raise more money, and they succeeded in raising at least three times more than ever before (and repeated that for several years). Much more than that, though, she brought a community together for laughs and fun. She was not a business leader, but was a true leader of people.

My mom possessed an extraordinary gift for writing notes and sending cards. While I may not have inherited her knack for selecting the perfect card (she could spend hours in the Hallmark store!), I have embraced her cherished habit of sending handwritten notes.

In this age of technology, texts, and emails, a handwritten note has the unique power to stand out. I did not know it at the time, but two friends of mine went through years of cancer treatments; after my mom passed, they told me she had sent them weekly cards and notes for several years!

Countless individuals have shared with me how my mom's notes and cards provided them comfort during times of illness and loss, and brought joy in moments of celebration. She had an exceptional ability to remember significant dates that many overlooked, such as anniversaries of miscarriages or the passing of loved ones. Her unwavering kindness and thoughtful gestures brought solace and unity to many lives. In my view, my mom's superpowers were communication, bringing people together, connectedness, and creativity – skills that she masterfully employed and which I have strived to embrace in my own life.

ME

Of course, I'm not perfect, but I do understand my superpowers. When things don't go well, it's almost always because I wasn't focused on using them or because I wasn't respecting the superpowers of others around me. Of course, we do not always know the superpowers of others, which makes it a bit more complicated. To address this uncertainty, I encourage everyone around me – my team members, my family, and my friends – to take the CliftonStrengths® assessment. I felt proud when my children asked for CliftonStrengths® codes for their friends and partners.

I use my strengths and superpowers almost every day, but it took a lot of practice to get there. It's easy to assume that your strengths are instinctively utilized at all times. However, that's not always the case. We don't always use them in a positive or productive way. For example, my strength in positivity often leads me to see the best in others and situations, but it can also make me overlook obvious obstacles. I must deliberately harness my strengths to fully unleash my superpowers' potential.

My superpowers work best when I use my strengths to positively influence people, or projects, or situations. A few examples of how I've used my strengths in a productive manner are:

I led the HR Indiana SHRM conference for many years. We had almost 2,000 attendees and spent over a year planning the event. We had successful conferences before I took charge, so I had a strong base to begin with, but I used my influencing strengths to build strong committees and let them do their thing. My strategic strengths helped me to look forward and not be afraid to try new ideas and take different paths. My positivity (sometimes to a fault) drove me to keep us moving forward – even during COVID – with the very best of intentions!

Building my business, Purple Ink LLC, is one of my proudest business accomplishments. I wish I could tell you it was all thanks to my strategic powers (strategic, futuristic, input). I know those helped, but the knowledge that I never wrote a business plan may lead you to believe otherwise! I think it was totally my positivity (#3), my self-assurance (#8), my communication (#9) and my "woo" (#7) that helped me get started (along with powerful mentors). Using all 10 of my core strengths helped keep the business growing!

Midway through my career, I mentored a receptionist who was looking for more challenging work. We developed trust in one another, and I began to delegate more assignments to her and teach her human resource skills, building her competencies and confidence. She later moved onto the HR team, was promoted to a recruiting manager, and, eventually, became the director of recruiting.

I was an HR generalist when I started my business, and, admittedly, it took me too long to hone my skills. Once there was a strong team in place, I asked myself, *What is the work I want to do more of, what am I energized by, and where do I find my joy?* I was then able to hone my influencer strengths as a business owner, business developer, trainer, speaker, and author. I can – and love – to influence all day long!

On a personal note, I became a better mother when I understood my children's superpowers. "Woo" is one of my influencing strengths, so I love the challenge of meeting new people, making new connections, and winning them over. All three of my children are "relators" who enjoy close relationships with a smaller group of friends. Before I knew their strengths, I insisted on inviting their entire class and most of the neighborhood to their birthday parties, even though they would ask me to just invite a few close friends. Who had the best time at their parties? Of course, it was me and not them!

It's significantly easier to be exponentially better in areas in which you already excel than to focus your time and energy on areas that you are not good at, don't enjoy, or that weigh you down.

ACTIONS TO ELEVATE <u>YOUR</u> SUPERPOWERS!

Once you name your superpowers and use the observations of others to claim them, you can concentrate on elevating them. Once again, that took years of practice for me, so it's not to be taken lightly. How can you elevate them to their fullest power? I have some ideas:

1. FOCUS ON YOUR STRENGTHS

Do what you do well and seek out opportunities to do it more! Once you have zoned in on your superpowers, continue to focus on them. It's significantly easier to be exponentially better in areas in which you already excel than to focus your time and energy on areas that you are not good at, don't enjoy, or that weigh you down.

I recently coached a senior leader. He shared with me that he constantly felt guilty for not being a good executor of his own ideas. Once he understood that his powers were in strategy and influence, he was able to erase his guilt and feel significantly more energized in his work. He had built a team of people who were focused on executing his ideas, and they were excelling. This new understanding of himself and his team allowed him to stay out of their way (which was empowering to them). While it is important to recognize and address our weaknesses, our exponential power lies in the areas where we exceed expectations. By taking this approach, this leader discovered more joy in his work!

2. LEARN

Seek out excellent training opportunities throughout your career. Whether it's technical or leadership training, hands-on learning with strong mentors, or attending company-wide programs tailored to your level, take every chance to grow your skills. Make a commitment to lifelong learning, regardless of age or career stage. Always strive to expand your knowledge and develop your abilities. I recently supported one of my teammates as she earned a certification in emotional intelligence. She has used what she learned as an opportunity to grow as an individual and leader, to train our team on the fundamentals and power of understanding our own emotional intelligence. She is also training and coaching our clients on this topic – a win-win all around!

3. LISTEN TO PODCASTS

Podcasts are a fantastic, cost-effective way to learn and educate yourself and others. Consider listening to a diverse range of podcasts to broaden your knowledge on various subjects. I consistently have podcasts in my queue on business and leadership, religious teachings, and world and local news. Engaging with podcasts can enhance your conversational skills, keep you up to date on current topics, and provide fresh perspectives. They are a versatile tool that can fit into your daily routine, whether you're commuting, exercising, or even doing household chores. Listening to podcasts allows you to multitask and make the most of your time, turning otherwise mundane activities into opportunities for personal growth and development.

4. READ

Reading is a powerful tool that can significantly contribute to personal growth and education. It opens doors to new perspectives, enhances knowledge, and fosters critical thinking. I've always been an avid reader (reading over 100 books per year), but when I started my business in 2010, I set a goal to only read business books for one year. Yes, some were painful, but I learned so much. In 2011, my goal was to read half business and half nonfiction books. I no longer set reading goals and read mysteries, thrillers, romance, biographies of all kinds, business, and a few self-help books. Engaging with diverse reading materials sharpens cognitive abilities such as comprehension, analytical thinking, and memory retention, and encourages a deeper level of thinking and problem-solving.

Is time or motivation an obstacle to setting a reading habit for you? Consider joining a book club or utilizing technology such as e-books, audiobooks, or reading apps. Select books that align with your personal or professional goals. Reading with a specific purpose in mind can be more fulfilling and impactful.

SUMMARY

My goal in this chapter is to empower you to be better. It is not to encourage you to be more like me, or my mom, or Roxy, it's to be like *you*. . . at your best. Understanding your strengths, talents, and gifts – truly understanding them – allows you to know what you do best and aim to do more of it. The more you intentionally use your strengths, the more likely you are to find joy in your life, to be more productive, to have more energy, and to be excited and energized by what you are doing. I hope to empower you to find your superpowers – and discover more joy!

CHAPTER 2

You-Powered: Charting the Course to Career Joy

Jill Lehman

ACC, CPC, ELI-MP Certified Coach, Speaker,
and Human Resources Consultant
Founder & CEO, Evolve HR Group

 linkedin.com/in/jilllehman

 evolvehrgroup.com

Jill is a human resources executive who has held executive roles within a diverse array of organizations, ranging from global enterprises to privately held companies.

At Evolve HR Group, she serves as its founder, CEO, and a senior advisor with a proven track record of helping organizations craft and execute people-focused strategies that enable the achievement of both business and talent goals.

Jill's HR expertise is in strategy, organizational and talent development and transformation. Jill understands that the key to unlock growth and productivity is through developing sound people strategies, processes, and leaders skilled in fostering a people-first culture: the core elements needed to fuel agile, productive, growth-minded, and future-ready organizations.

As a coach, Jill works with clients across a variety of industries and career levels with the goals of helping clients discover their potential, own their careers, and align their personal and professional goals to achieve success.

Jill is an accredited CPC through iPEC and ACC from the International Coaching Federation, as well as an Energy Leadership Index (ELI) master practitioner. Her coaching engagements are with private clients, corporations, and universities. She received recognition as one of Indianapolis's Top 15 Coaches from Influence Digest and as HR Professional of the Year from the Indiana Chamber of Commerce.

I see you and I have been you. You wonder how to get the promotion or the dream job you've envisioned. Why does it appear to be the good fortune of some but, for you, it feels out of reach? You may wonder, *How do I get my name to land on the corporate wheel of opportunities?* As an HR professional and career coach, I can promise you that you are not alone. I've spent decades coaching, training, and building corporate employment brands focused on this topic.

Take Robin as an example. Robin is a coaching client of mine. Robin went to the college her parents suggested she attend and studied accounting because that was what her father went to school for and comprised the work he had done for a living. He had told her it was a good, stable job with good pay. Turn the clock ahead 10 years. Robin works in an accounting firm where she has been employed since she graduated college. Robin feels she earns an average wage for an accountant, but less than her goal income, and she has added responsibilities that accumulated over the years as she worked her way up from an associate to accounting manager. Her employer convinced her to pursue her MBA at a school they recommended. Robin was told by her manager that getting an MBA was a common path that could create new job opportunities for her in senior accounting leadership roles and a worthwhile investment in her individual development. Robin, feeling unfulfilled in her work as an accountant, decided to take her employer up on this opportunity and pursued her MBA so she could continue to have opportunities in the firm. Can you see the pattern emerging?

In our careers, we often begin to function on autopilot. Letting the winds and the highway (that is, cruise control) take us where they think we should be. That is the opposite of what truly benefits us. Intentional career navigation and our "best fit" destinations can be reached when we become "you-powered."

What does it mean to be *you-powered?* Think of it like taking the wheel and charting the course to get to your career destination. You naturally do this when planning vacations, but when it comes to our careers, we often leave it up to others or follow along for the ride.

So now that I have your attention, what does it take to be *you-powered?* Being *you-powered* at its core involves giving yourself permission to chart the path to your desired career destination. There are a few essentials you need when taking the wheel, which I will discuss in this chapter. *Claiming your power, being intentional,* and what I often refer to in coaching is *mastering oneself* in the form of self-discovery, career reflection, self-advocacy, and self-accountability.

RECLAIM YOUR POWER

For too many women, careers aren't built – they unfold. We find ourselves making decisions by circumstance, based on the expectations of others, often led by our own fears or the biases we face in the workplace. We sit back and wait for the promotion to be earned rather than pursue it. We graciously accept roles provided to us rather than curate them to fulfill our desires. When it comes to compensation, we hope the raise is a good one, rather than negotiating it. And when we take a moment to pause and reflect, or in some cases before we realize it, we are on a path we rarely choose. Our career path is shaped by the forces around us.

Why is it that women often unknowingly allow others to dictate their career? Is it because a well-meaning parent or mentor nudges us into a "safe" role instead of a stretch opportunity? Because a manager assumes we wouldn't want a leadership position due to family obligations or the extra effort that will be required? Maybe it's because we assume we need to take a backseat to allow others in our lives to advance their careers, or we worry our children will be less than perfect if we pursue our careers, fearing we can't have it all. Even the best-intentioned company's cultures often play into the societal narratives about what women "should" prioritize in subtle ways.

Challenging the assumptions or limiting beliefs placed on us feels daunting. We often grow comfortable with them and patiently wait for recognition, or, better yet, for our name to finally land on the career opportunity wheel, rather than charting the course to the career we desire. We accommodate and internalize doubts that are given to us. Sound familiar? That's what happened to Robin.

When we reclaim our power, we give ourselves permission to take the wheel and chart the course on the journey to career joy. When women become *you-powered*, we make career choices with purpose, as opposed to accepting the jobs or careers given to us, by truly owning our path to the work and career that excites and fulfills us. We choose to move past the limiting beliefs and assumptions imposed on us and instead define what success is on our terms. We no longer wait for our name to come up on the career opportunity wheel or take the bypass to something others view as satisfactory. We put *you-power* in motion to create the life and work we envision. Sounds more rewarding and exciting, doesn't it?

When reclaiming and moving to a *you-powered* career, it is not an overnight transformation; it requires a series of intentional decisions. Start by asking yourself:

Am I actively making career choices, or am I letting them happen to me? Am I doing work that fulfills me or am I playing small or safe in my career? What would I do if I wasn't worried about disappointing others or taking risks? What am I good at, and what do I really enjoy doing? What am I not so good at, which I need to work on to get where I want to go?

BE INTENTIONAL: HARNESS YOUR INTERNAL GPS

When you are intentional in your career, you make conscious, strategic decisions rather than letting circumstances or others dictate the path. You shift from a career of convenience, or fear of uncertainty, and riding in the backseat while others drive, to actively shaping and building your career destination. When you own the journey, you can unlock opportunities that align with your ambitions, strengths, passions, and goals.

On the road to being more intentional, I teach my clients to start with clarity. Know what you genuinely want, not just in terms of job titles or salaries, but the kind of work you enjoy, are good at, and that excites and fulfills you. Ask yourself: *What impact do I want to make? What kind of projects light me up? What values do I want my work to reflect? What aspects of my job would make it ideal?* Without this foundation, it's easy for us to drift into roles that feel safe but uninspiring and take the wrong opportunities that derail us or allow us to stay in positions simply because they're comfortable.

Once you have clarity, the next step is intentional decision-making. Decision-making, in this context, relates to how you go about getting where you want to go. This could mean seeking out projects that build the skills you need for your next move, networking with the right people, working to position yourself and ask for leadership or specialized roles before you feel completely ready, seeking out necessary training or education, and figuring out logistics and/or family obligations so you have the bandwidth you need to focus. I often hear my mentor's wise words in my mind, that "Growth rarely happens when we are in a passive state; it's the result of our deliberate actions to make it happen."

Another area of intentionality that I discuss with my clients, which is equally important, is setting boundaries. If you don't define what success and fulfillment look like for *you* and protect it like you do other things in your life that you cherish, it's easy to get swept up in what others expect or need from you before caring for and nurturing our own needs. Before you know it, without boundaries, you take on extra responsibilities without recognition, stay in a job out of loyalty rather than growth, take jobs you fear saying "no" to, or sacrifice your goals or well-being for others. When these happen, you may feel the pressure and give up because you are overwhelmed or move back to "career autopilot." Intentional career planning includes saying "no" to what doesn't serve you and making room for what does.

Being intentional isn't just about career achievement: it's about finding *joy* in your career because you have intentionally built it around your passions, strengths, and the type of work that fuels you and leads to a fulfilling life.

When you are intentional, you treat your career as something you shape, not something that happens to you. It's about making empowered, informed choices that align with your ambitions and values.

Now that we have the frame on your car you'll take on your journey to a *you-powered* career, let's ignite the engine. This, in my coaching process, is where mastering the *you-powered* gears comes in.

THE YOU-POWERED GEARS

1. SELF-AWARENESS

When you take time to understand yourself and then jump in the driver's seat, it's powerful. Self-awareness gives you clarity about who you are, what you want, and why you make the choices you make. Without self-awareness, you risk drifting through life reacting to circumstances rather than intentionally shaping your path. Ultimately, you will show up in energies and in ways that can work against you, thus preventing you from creating a life and a career that feels meaningful.

Understanding yourself allows you to improve, build, and grow as an individual and in your career. When you recognize your triggers, fears, patterns, and limiting beliefs, you will become better at managing your thoughts and emotions instead of being controlled by them. When you master managing your emotions, you will become better at managing your energy levels, your mindset, and how you show up. You will respond to situations with greater resilience, reduced stress, and fewer impulsive reactions. It deepens your empathy, making it easier to build strong, authentic relationships. The more you understand yourself, the better you can communicate, set boundaries, and cultivate meaningful connections that uplift you. See where I am going with this, based on our earlier discussions in this chapter?

Personal growth is another key benefit of self-awareness. By identifying your limiting beliefs and unconscious habits, you will gain the power to break negative cycles and replace them with healthier patterns. This leads to greater confidence, meaning you will no longer need external validation to feel worthy. You begin to trust yourself more; you begin to take bold steps toward your dreams and embrace challenges as opportunities to grow. The journey of self-awareness isn't always easy, but it's one of the most rewarding paths you can take.

When you understand yourself, it unlocks the freedom to live with more intention and work with the world around you to co-create opportunities. This sense of alignment will bring with it a deep sense of personal fulfillment that taking a backseat to your life and career can't provide. The more you invest in yourself, the more you can create a life and career that feels rich, vibrant, and uniquely yours.

2. CAREER DISCOVERY

A career built on other people's validation or while remaining in cruise control might lead to surface success (think title or financial rewards), but it's rarely fulfilling. The most powerful and rewarding career success comes from the process of discovery. Taking the time to explore and validate what brings you joy, increases your energy, and plays to your strengths has a greater likelihood of leading to career success and satisfaction. At the same time, knowing what depletes your energy and doesn't align to who you are and what brings you joy is just as valuable of an insight.

When in career discovery, you need to take an honest inventory of your knowledge, skills, and abilities and how they align with your desired career goals. Ask yourself, what needs to be shored up or invested in to help me get on the road to where I want to go? What are the gains versus the pains when making job or career changes, and am I comfortable with them? What are my negotiables versus my non-negotiables when it comes to my job or career? In what type of work environment, culture, and leadership will I thrive?

On your trip to career success, I view career self-discovery as making sure you have the right mode of transportation and checking that it's in working order to get you where you want to be.

My clients often hear me say that self-discovery requires you to shed outdated – *and* other people's – definitions of success and embrace what truly excites, energizes, and aligns with you. Whether it means finding happiness as an individual contributor, leading a team, launching a business – well, the possibilities are endless. What I am trying to say is that when there is joy in your career, it reflects who you are, not just what is expected of you or assigned by others.

Thinking back to my client, Robin, her education, career field, and travel at this point in her career had been designated by others, as opposed to her giving herself permission to take the wheel. Imagine the possibilities when you take the time to explore who you are and what type of work leads to a career where you thrive.

3. SELF-ADVOCACY

Career self-advocacy is all about boldly owning your value in the workplace, in your educational pursuits, and, frankly, anywhere that touches your career ambitions. It means speaking up for yourself – whether it's negotiating a raise, asking for that promotion, changing careers, or setting boundaries that protect your focus, energy, and general well-being. It's having confidence in yourself and being intentional in the pursuit of your career goals.

Often in my coaching practice, the biggest challenge with self-advocacy that my clients have is they don't believe they have the skills, abilities, or they feel it's too late. I am here to tell you it's not too late, and rarely does anyone have all the skills and abilities they need for a role or project. What it does take is, let me say it again, some intentionality.

Clients can self-advocate when they know what they bring to the table in their careers. What are your top strengths? Are you able to demonstrate them? We discuss the importance of having a voice and speaking up. Don't wait for the opportunity wheel to land on your name to be recognized; instead, make your interest and why you are a great candidate known.

Another common challenge is pursuing opportunities and actions outside of your comfort zone. Raise your hand for challenging projects, leadership roles, and learning opportunities. Curate experiences and get creative in finding ways to get the knowledge, skills, and capabilities you need to get where you want to go. Learn to set boundaries to ensure you stay in alignment with your goals. Another wonderful way to advocate is to build and leverage relationships. Find allies, mentors, coaches, and sponsors who can help you along your journey by providing guidance, being your accountability partners, and helping open doors.

Bottom line, if you don't advocate, you leave your career trajectory in someone else's hands. What's the biggest challenge you face with self-advocacy?

For my client, Robin, her biggest challenge was feeling stuck, holding limiting beliefs about her abilities, not knowing what she wanted to do for a career, and being comfortable, yet unsatisfied, with the pay and stable work, lacking engagement and generally unhappy with her current career journey.

4. SELF-ACCOUNTABILITY

Career self-accountability is the no-excuses, take-charge mindset that puts you in the driver's seat of your professional journey. It's the difference between waiting for opportunities and creating them, or blaming external factors and owning your growth, decisions, and results.

When you get to this accountability phase in my career coaching practice, you work first and foremost to set the vision and crystal-clear goals. If you don't know where you're going, and how you are going to get there, you'll end up nowhere. Gaining forward momentum is key to sticking with most things. To make goals attainable and realistic, break them into actionable steps. For example, you have identified the need to learn project management skills. Consider breaking the goal into the following: research what specific project management skills you are looking to improve. Do you need training or a certification for your desired career goal? The next action step is researching training providers that offer what you are looking for, followed by signing up for the course. Then the final step is completing the class by a designated date.

Track your progress and measure results. The old saying is what gets measured gets done. The *you-powered* career journey is all about what is planned intentionally and focused on, and how it can bring the results you desire. Along the road, remember to celebrate your progress and reflect on lessons learned or recalibrate when you fall short.

My client, Robin, has walked the path to becoming *you-powered*. She put in the hard work to explore her career goals and what needed to be changed or put in place to get there. She is showing up for herself, challenging herself, and has created a clear, actionable plan charting the route to where she is headed. She no longer shows up for work going through the motions and feeling stuck or that her career is in the hands of others. She is happily working in a role where her accounting skills come in handy, but her focus now is dedicated to her new career in property management. That is, she is now masterfully aligning her strengths and experiences, and being intentional, to land her *you-powered*-fueled dream job!

THE FAST LANE TO SUCCESS

Now that you have reclaimed your career journey and have the tools to be *you-powered*, remember that while having a supportive tribe around you is valuable, the primary ingredient in career success is **you**. Stop waiting for validation when you can be in the driver's seat, mapping out and bringing to life the career of your dreams!

CHAPTER 3

All's Well That Ends

Kerrie M. Weinzapfel

Writer and Speaker

linkedin.com/in/kerrie-weinzapfel-844aba20

my52todo.com

kerrieweinzapfel@gmail.com

Kerrie M. Weinzapfel spent her career in the accounting and legal services fields. She has over 25 years of experience in management, including serving as a chief operating officer at Farmer Scott Ozete Robinson & Schmitt LLP, firm administrator at Bamberger Foreman Oswald and Hahn, LLP, and operations manager at a regional CPA firm. As a certified public accountant, she has extensive experience managing financial and accounting functions. Her experience also included being responsible for all business office functions, including business development, compensation programs, employee training and benefits, human resources, information technology, professional development initiatives, professional recruitment, public relations, and strategic planning.

After a 36-year career, Kerrie recently retired. She now spends her time travelling and writing.

T he famous saying "all's well that ends well" is certainly true. Hopefully, this rings true in your personal life and in your career. There are many joyful endings in our careers. We end one position for another due to a promotion or an exciting new opportunity. We move and begin a career with a new employer. We joyfully complete a career and transition to the long-dreamed-of retirement. These endings "end well" because we plan for them. We set goals, set timetables, and make the decision to take the leap.

But not all endings "end well." Not all endings are of our own choosing. Positions are eliminated. Businesses merge or are acquired. Leadership changes. Company culture morphs into one with which we are no longer satisfied. We grow out of our role or experience no upward mobility. Our situations, needs, or desires change.

When professional changes occur, especially in situations not of our choosing, it can be difficult to find joy. It can feel unfair, frustrating, even hopeless. In times like these, I believe it is especially important to look for joy in your work and your workplace. You may have to search, but it is better emotionally to focus on the good, rather than dwell on the bad.

To me, joy and happiness are two different emotions. Happiness is more fleeting than joy. It is experiential. I experience it in the moment, but it ends when the experience is over. For example, you might feel happy when eating ice cream. That happy feeling probably ends when the dish is empty. Joy is a deeper, longer-lasting feeling. Joy stays after the experience is over. Joy makes the days, weeks, and years better. It allows you to face difficult situations because you know the challenge is temporary. An example of joy is the feeling I experience when spending time with my adult children. I still feel that emotion long after the visit is over. Perhaps you feel joy when you develop a project at work and see it through to success. This joy sustains you when it is time to tackle the next hurdle.

Like me, you may have worked for several employers during your professional career. At each stop in my career, I have experienced great joy. I also experienced heartbreak, failure, anger, frustration, and disappointment. Each of my roles ended for a different reason. Two of the three were transitions I did not want. These transitions forced me to look for joy when things did not work out according to my plans. While it would have been easy to wallow in negative emotions, it is healthier to focus on the positive and on joy. I believe our careers and our lives are better when we focus our energy on joy.

A CAREER ROADMAP

Do you have a person in your family or community who inspired you early in life? Did you map out your career based on your observation of someone else's path? My earliest professional role model was my dad. I have immense respect for my father and envisioned my career path to look much like his. My father worked for the same company for his entire career. I thought that was what you did. You begin a job after college, work hard, and get promotions along the way. You and your coworkers build something really great together. After a 40-year career at this same place, you retire. During retirement, you meet your former colleagues for coffee and donuts at the local breakfast hangout. This was the life I envisioned for myself. Did you envision your career path taking a familiar road?

PREPARE TO MERGE, LANE ENDS

While I learned many lessons at each stop in my career, my first career taught me that while things may not always go according to plan, you can move on to equally great (or even better) things. I began my career at a regional CPA firm. As I had planned, I started as a staff accountant, earned promotions along the way, and was ultimately promoted to the role of operations manager. I loved this role and this place with all my heart. My boss was supportive of me and my flexible schedule. I felt accomplished at work, had the flexibility I desired for my family, and everything was moving along, just as I had planned.

After about 10 years with the firm, the firm began merger discussions with another regional firm. I knew a merger would create change, but I was ready to embrace this change. Unfortunately, the operations manager position was not common in the industry and was not going to continue after the merger. I had two choices: I could return to client service, or I could accept a buyout. What do you do when you have the dream job at the dream place and that job disappears? It was difficult for me to embrace the fact that this was no longer going to be the right place for me.

I went through a real period of grief when I made my decision to leave. Maybe you, too, have left a position due to changes from an acquisition. Although I was only in my early 30s, I had planned my retirement party in my mind. The thought of having to restart my career somewhere that would clearly be inferior to the perfect job with the perfect people was just flat out depressing. To say that I felt like the joy was sucked out of my professional life would be an understatement.

My parents instilled many important lessons in me, and at this time, I had to rely on some of those lessons. At first, it took a lot of energy to show up at the office each day with a positive attitude. I was raised to be a team player, even when that meant I was not going to personally benefit. I was absolutely not going to be anything other than a cheerleader for this merger, but I will tell you there were days when it was really difficult. I realized I had to change my focus from what I had lost and what might have been, to finding joy in what I had accomplished and the good I could still do for the people who would continue at the firm.

> ....
>
> Your joy and professional development require investing the time to make intentional and thought-filled decisions, not just easy ones.
>
> ....

I poured my heart into my final project, a new office building for the firm, making it the most functional and beautiful place I could. I felt an incredible sense of joy when I watched everyone on move-in day. I wanted the people I cared about to continue to be successful. I also felt joy when I came back to the office later as a client. I was able to reflect on things I had accomplished, like being an early adopter of an alternative career path and helping pave the way for other women to work flexible schedules. I was able to celebrate accomplishments, such as initiatives I had captained. I still get a feeling of joy when I see the success of people I worked with, many of whom I hired. While I was incredibly sad to see it end, all was still well.

If you find yourself in a similar situation, one in which your position is eliminated due to department changes, business closures, or mergers, you may have a decision to make. If you are offered a move to a different role, I encourage you to take the time to make the decision that is right for you. It can feel less overwhelming to stay, even with a less satisfactory role. Don't settle. Your joy and professional development require investing the time to make intentional and thought-filled decisions, not just easy ones. Moving to a new role within the same company may be the right decision for you. Take the time to truly explore the internal opportunity, as well as external options. Ask yourself:

- Will I be professionally challenged if I stay?
- Am I staying because it is emotionally safer than making a change?
- What does the perfect job look like, and does this opportunity check those boxes?
- What do I gain by continuing with my current employer? What could I gain from other opportunities?
- If the change is due to a merger or acquisition, how will the culture change? Is this new culture the right fit for me?

If you decide to make a change and move to a new employer, don't focus on what you have lost. When my children experienced disappointment, I always told them, set a timetable to wallow in your sadness. Maybe it is an hour, or a day. After that, you need to move on and focus your attention on the future. You will live a better life if you celebrate the joy and accomplishments of the past and use those to motivate you as you plan for the future. Ask yourself:

- What projects were your brainchildren?
- What personal development goals did you set and achieve?
- How were you able to mentor others?
- How were you able to impact the productivity and success of your department or employer?

These questions will help you embrace the joy of what you accomplished. They will also help you refine your resume for your job search.

CAUTION, DIVIDED HIGHWAY

Having learned the lesson that life doesn't always go according to our plan, I moved on to the second stop in my career. I started a new role as HR manager with an expanding law firm, ultimately becoming the firm administrator. In the previous section, I mentioned that "the thought of having to restart my career somewhere that would clearly be inferior to the perfect job with the perfect people was just flat out depressing." It turns out there could be more than one place that turned out to be the perfect job, with the perfect people. Have you ever been pleasantly surprised to find you were wrong and that starting over was actually a good thing?

The managing partner was a great strategist, a fantastic lawyer, and an even better human. He taught me the value of patience as a strategy. The lawyers and staff cared passionately about the work we did and each other. A coworker at the firm introduced me to the concept of **"all's well that ends."** I was not there the first time he said it, so I have never known if he misspoke or said it intentionally, but the concept stuck. When we had a difficult situation or a project failed, we would move on, joyful that at least it was over. We would put that experience in our rearview mirror and focus on the road ahead. Can you remember a time in your career or personal life when you were glad simply because an experience ended, and it was time to move forward?

During my years at the firm, we grew to have multiple offices across the state, often through mergers. If you have experienced meshing cultures resulting from mergers, you know that this can be challenging. In my final year with the firm, the cultural challenges we faced became a significant divide.

When faced with difficulty, what is your standard approach? I have always embraced the idea of being "in this together." I believe that all things in life are cyclical, so a difficult situation won't last forever. If we all pull together and share the pain, we can move forward together and share in the future success.

How do you face each day when you are in the middle of a struggle? I went to work every day believing this was the day everyone would join together, and I was so incredibly frustrated when they didn't. I eventually came to realize that those who did not share my outlook were equally frustrated with me and my approach to resolving issues.

After one particularly challenging day, I began to share my frustrations at home. Our son said something that profoundly impacted my life. He told me that I had become "a whirling dervish of anger."

Wow! Like the proverbial frog put into the pot of water who doesn't hop out as it gradually gets to a boiling point, I didn't realize the impact the lengthy and ultimately unwinnable culture war was having on me. While I would have told you I still had joy in

> I read a quote at some point that said, "Don't let your loyalty keep you in situations that break your heart."

my job, it simply was not true. The joy I felt was remembered joy, not current joy. I simply had to face the fact that this was no longer the right place for me. I submitted my resignation that week.

I read a quote at some point that said, "Don't let your loyalty keep you in situations that break your heart." I realized that my heart was broken by the constant conflict and my loyalty to the firm was making me stay. Have you ever overstayed in a position due to loyalty to a person or place? The reality was that the firm I was loyal to no longer existed and I was not the right person to resolve this conflict.

Resigning after thinking about it for less than 48 hours is probably the scariest thing I have ever done in my career, but I knew I had to pull the band-aid off quickly while I was brave enough to do it. Resigning without having a new job already lined up was a bold move for me. Not one I necessarily recommend, either. Please consult your financial advisor first!

I can also say that making the decision allowed me to return to a place of joy at work. I did not want to leave the firm in a bind, so I agreed to stay to transition my work to the incoming employee. Just like at my previous job, this time gave me the opportunity to find joy in reflecting on what I had accomplished. I could be joyful with coworkers who did not see things the way I did because it no longer mattered. We were not adversaries. I could just appreciate them as people. I could even find humor in some of the culture war issues. I felt a renewed sense of freedom and joy because I had taken back control of my life, my future, and my decisions. There are times in life when we can simply feel joy because a difficult time in our life is behind us, and this was that time for me. I could find joy in it because all's well that ends.

Are you in a spot in your career where you are constantly frustrated, even to the point of anger? If so, take the time to really examine why.

- Are my frustrations internal or external?
- Do I have the tools I need to resolve internal frustrations? Do I need training or mentoring to develop new skills to resolve the issues?
- If the frustrations are external, do I have the skills, relationships, or authority to work to resolve them?
- How long can I live with this level of frustration before it impacts my work, my health, and my relationships? Is it a sacrifice I should make or am willing to make?

Deep introspection and analysis of your situation might help you decide the merits of working through the frustration compared to the value of exploring other opportunities. There are times in life where we determine that there is more out there. . . and it is time to move forward to find joy somewhere else.

CHECK SPEED, EXIT AHEAD

If you have ever left a position without having secured a new role, you probably started the search with some fear and anxiety and then moved on to the business of finding one. When investigating new avenues, do you feel enthusiastic? At the time, I had spent my entire career in management of professional services firms. I was now able to research opportunities in other industries, like banking and manufacturing. While it can be frightening, there can be joy and excitement in being open to previously unexplored possibilities.

In an interesting turn of events, a new law firm was created by some of my former coworkers, and they asked me to join them as their chief operating officer. The final seven years of my career have been so professionally rewarding. The challenge of helping create something from nothing is exhilarating, frightening, and rewarding. I feel so much joy about what we created together and those with whom I did it. As with all things, this, too, is coming to an end. This time, the timing was completely of my choosing, as I am retiring.

Do you spend time thinking about your retirement? Making the decision to retire is an incredibly joyful time. There is joy in celebrating your accomplishments. There is joy in planning a future without the time constraints of work. There is joy in completing bucket list goals. You might also feel some apprehension. Having recently retired, I can tell you that the decision to retire is an emotional one. As my husband and I came to our final decision on timing, we realized that we had been totally focused on a monetary goal. We had not really invested any time in thinking about the emotional impact of retiring.

If you are starting to think about the end of your career and retirement, I encourage you to devote some time to thinking about the following:

- How will I continue to challenge myself mentally?
- What will I actually do each day? Losing the routine of going to a place can create a sense of being untethered. This can be uncomfortable for some people.

- Do I have an identity beyond my professional accomplishments? If not, how will this impact my feelings of self-worth? What do I need to do to expand my identity?
- What will bring me joy each day?

THE END OF THE ROAD

I believe experiencing joy at work is essential to satisfaction at work and in life. We can feel joy at work when we accomplish our personal and professional goals, help others to achieve their goals, express thankfulness, and do meaningful things. When your situation changes and you lose that sense of joy, I hope you invest the time in yourself to determine the cause and empower yourself to find it again. When you determine the time is right to end your career and enter retirement, I hope, as you leave the office one final time, you feel that "all's well that ends well!"

CHAPTER 4

Just

MeChelle Callen

Author, Coach, Speaker

🌐 mechellecallen.com

in linkedin.com/in/mechellecallen

f facebook.com/mechellemcallen

📷 instagram.com/mechellecallen

MeChelle Callen is an author, coach, and speaker dedicated to helping women find their voice, claim space, and secure their seat at the table. She challenges norms that minimize women's contributions and dismantles limiting language, including the habitual use of "just."

With three decades in HR, organizational development, leadership, and DEIB, plus 15 years as an executive, MeChelle has shaped organizational cultures and created award-winning programs recognized by Training Magazine's Top 125 and Brandon Hall. A sought-after speaker, she has presented at the SHRM Annual Conference, HR Indiana, and the Women's VIP Conference. She holds an MBA, SPHR, and SHRM-SCP, drawing on experience in nonprofit management, healthcare, commercial real estate, and financial services.

Her dedication to transformation inspires a new generation of leaders. MeChelle envisions a world where women continue to unapologetically step into leader roles, fiercely advocate for themselves and one another, and intentionally ensure every voice is heard and every potential is realized.

MeChelle's mission and work are driven by her devotion to her family and her desire to shape a better world for them—and for generations to come.

Have you ever found yourself downplaying your accomplishments or dismissing your successes with subtle qualifiers, almost without noticing it? Or dimming the light of your efforts before anyone else has a chance to celebrate them?

I am an author. That simple statement – without hesitation or qualification – is a shift in how I view myself and my work. Yet, *just* a few short months ago, I found myself saying, "I'm *just* writing a chapter. I'm not an author." *Just* rolled off my tongue, and, to be honest, I didn't think twice about it initially. However, that small yet significant slip of language forced me to confront a deeper issue: Why was I minimizing my own achievements? Why was I reducing the value of my work with a single, unnecessary word *just?*

Now, I'm one of those people who, when a word or a phrase gets stuck in my head, I hear it everywhere. It's like the car-buying experience, where, if you decide you are going to buy a black Jeep Cherokee, suddenly there are black Jeeps everywhere. In reality, there are not more Jeeps on the road, but as your awareness is heightened, your focus changes. I began to intentionally focus on the word *just*, and then, to no surprise, I heard it everywhere.

"I'm *just* an employee; I can't do anything about it."

"I'm *just* an average student, no grad school for me."

"I'm *just* the free speaker."

"I'm *just* one person; I can't make a difference."

"I'm *just* a mom."

"I'm *just* a volunteer."

"I'm *just* on the JV squad."

"I'm *just* a small business owner."

"I'm *just* lucky!"

I heard it over and over again and more often than not I heard women adding the adverb *just* to their role, their work, their opinions, and their accomplishments. Women – smart, capable, accomplished women – were using *just* to shrink themselves, to sideline their contributions, to make their presence seem less significant.

Just is an adverb that can mean "barely," "by a little," or "no more than." *Just* is a thief! It steals confidence. It diminishes accomplishments. It subtly communicates that what you do, what you contribute, and who you are is somehow not enough. And it must end!

These conversations led me on a journey of personal and professional reflection and to have more meaningful conversations with women. I wondered, why is it that, as women, we sometimes feel the need to take up less space – to not live in the empowerment that we possess? Why is it safer for you to step back than it is for you to step up and into your authority and power?

· · · · · · · · · · · · · · · · · · · ·

Just is a thief!

· · · · · · · · · · · · · · · · · · · ·

I remember being a bold and boisterous child with no fear. Heck, I was the top cookie-selling girl scout for three years in a row (I still have my 1974 Top Sales Kangaroo button). In fourth grade, I organized my first grassroots protest against the town's department of transportation for paving our brick street (brick streets are the best for kickball when you know where to aim the ball). Looking back, I can only imagine the thoughts of the asphalt workers as they paved the street, and five kids marched up and down the sidewalk with our handmade cardboard box signs chanting, "*Stop!*" I don't think "*just*" was part of that little girl's vocabulary, so when did that change?

In speaking with other women, we realized it didn't happen to us all at once. It was the cues we received from others over time. The conditioning started early. You were told not to be too loud, not to take up too much space, not to be too opinionated, and not to be so noticeable.

I got in trouble for being too boisterous, too talkative, too much. . . I can still hear my mother saying "MeChelle, stop laughing like that – it isn't very ladylike." In a discussion with another female leader, she shared with me it was in her mid-thirties when she realized something she was taught as a young girl. She was taught it's not attractive to speak boldly – to be confident in yourself or laugh too loudly – it is too prideful.

Research indicates that women frequently downplay their accomplishments. This downplay is influenced by societal biases and internalized perceptions. A 2020 study from Harvard Business School found that, on average, men rated their performance at 61 out of 100, while women rated theirs at 46, despite similar actual performance levels. The phenomenon of "Tall Poppy Syndrome," where individuals are resented or undermined due to their success, disproportionately affects women. In fact, according to a 2023 study by Dr. Rumeet Billan, 87% of the women surveyed from 103 countries had experienced Tall Poppy Syndrome at work.

Impostor syndrome, which is characterized by persistent self-doubt and fear of being exposed as a fraud, is more prevalent among women. A 2024 survey by KPMG reported that 75% of U.S. women executives experienced impostor syndrome, leading them to downplay their achievements, which also hinders their career progression.

Additionally, societal expectations and gender stereotypes contribute to this behavior. Studies have shown that women often feel pressured to conform to nurturing roles, perceiving self-promotion as boastful or inappropriate. This internalized bias results in women being more likely to underestimate their performance and less likely to advocate for their successes compared to men.

As our experience and research demonstrate, these messages accumulate over time until we internalize them as our truth. You learn to step back instead of stepping forward. You learn to soften how you speak of your impact rather than owning it. I wonder how many of you are reading this right now, nodding your head as you remember having a similar experience at home or at school. This is a reminder that what you say to a child matters!

Words matter, and the way we frame our identity and achievements matter. To clarify, I have not spent my life or career being small and diminishing myself. In fact, over the course of time, I have channeled that young, boisterous girl and spent my career and my life in roles that required me to take up space, to lead with confidence, and to empower others to do the same. When the voice inside my head starts speaking trash, I have an array of ways to regain my bigness.

In 2018, I decided to run for the Indiana House of Representatives. There is no such thing as "*just* running for office." You must be prepared to step up and show up. I was campaigning, advocating, and making my voice and those who supported me heard. And yet, there were moments when that internal voice tried to creep in, where the self-doubt whispered, "Who do you think you are?"

The first big event was the official launch of my campaign. It took place in a town hall, occupied by nearly 150 supporters and one trash-talking voice in my head.

It was time for me to shut that voice down and pull out one of my tools from my toolbox... the "power pose!"

Before I took the stage, I stepped out into the back parking lot, started playing my empowerment hype music, and struck the power poses. You all know what I am talking about, and you know you want to get up right now and do it with me. Come on – get up and let's do it.

Feet shoulder-width apart, arms high in the air in a Y formation, and repeat these words, "You've got this!" Oh, one time isn't enough – you need to say it at least three times – "You've got this!" "You've got this!" "You've got this!"

Now drop those arms and put your hands on your hips and take a deep breath in, expanding that chest, and as you let out that breath, shout "*yes*" or whatever feels right for you. When I do this, I silence the trash-talking voice in my head, and I am ignited.

I used this technique on the campaign trail before big events to remind myself that I belonged in that space. That I was prepared for it. I was enough! Using these techniques gave me the confidence to take up space in rooms where I was the only female candidate, and to confidently address my opponent without hesitation or a qualifier when he asked me, "And what do you do— I mean, do you work outside the home?"

I still use this technique before going into big meetings or speaking engagements. Now maybe this isn't your thing, but I hope it will give you inspiration to consider how you can silence the trash-talking **"just"** voice in your head.

Another tool I employ when I need to silence the trash-talking, imposter syndrome voice is an "Empowerment Hype Playlist."

My hype playlist is entitled "I've Got A Song For That!" On it are the songs "I Am Woman," "Confident," "Fight Song," "Break My Soul," to name a few. Some days I jump in my car, windows down, sunroof open, and drive with the music so loud the car thumps and I'm singing loud and proud like Beyonce (even though I can't hold a tune). Music is empowering for me. What song would be your hype song? Send me the title so I can add it to the *Just-I Am* playlist I'm creating to share with readers.

Speaking of inspiration, many times, leaders are asked, "Who were/are your role models that inspire you to be the leader you are?" I have always admired strong women leaders throughout history who helped to change or are changing the world. Eight years ago, my children started a birthday tradition; each year, I receive a framed silhouette with the image and name of a famous woman that I admire. Today, I have a collage of silhouettes on my bedroom wall. They are referred to as the "Bad Ass Bunch." These women include:

Shirley Chisolm. In 1968, she became the first Black woman to be elected to the United States Congress and served seven terms. She was also the first Black female candidate to run as the Democratic Party's nominee for president.

Marsha P. Johnson, a gay liberation activist and one of the prominent figures in the Stonewall uprising of 1969. She was an important advocate for homeless LGBTQ+ youth and those affected by H.I.V. and AIDS, and fought for transgender rights.

Chief Justice Ruth Bader Ginsberg was the second woman ever to sit as a justice on the nation's highest court, where she served for 27 years. She co-founded the Women's Rights Project at the American Civil Liberties Union (ACLU). She was a trailblazer.

Other notable women present are Ida B. Wells, Amelia Earhart, Susan B. Anthony, Maya Angelou, Frida Kahlo, and more. Every morning when I roll out of bed, I look at those silhouettes and I am reminded that women can and have changed the world. They inspire me.

Always remember your leadership journey could be someone else's road map.

You might be asking, so why does this story matter to the overall concept of women as leaders? Let me finish this story by telling you about my 60th birthday. My family had a surprise party for me. One of my dearest friends, Patty, gave me a gift, and when I opened it, it took my breath away and made my eyes well up with tears. What was looking back at me was a framed silhouette of me! It was identical to the other women on my wall. Patty said, "When I look at you, I see a badass leader who is changing the world, and Meesh you inspire me." *Wow...*

This is why it is important to step into our power as women leaders. Not only for yourself! Others are watching you. While you may not think you are worthy or doing world-changing things, always remember your leadership journey could be someone else's road map. Perhaps your story is another's survival guide. Your work, your leadership, your life are inspiration for them and how they want to live their life. What you tell your team members matters; what you tell your significant other, your family, and your friends matters. What you tell yourself matters. Words matter, and the smaller you make yourself, the smaller you make others.

Women must lead from a place of power, stepping into their accomplishments without reservation. That starts with recognizing the language you use and how it shapes your self-perception. When you say, "I'm *just* . . ." you are not only downplaying your own value, but also setting a precedent for others to do the same. But here's the thing: leadership isn't about being small. It isn't about playing it safe. Women who lead must do so boldly, unapologetically, and without the crutch of qualifiers that undercut their power.

When women lead, we must lead from an intentional place of authenticity and be big – taking up space at the table both literally and figuratively. And you must be ready. I don't believe people are *just* lucky. I believe people are prepared, and when preparation and opportunity align, it is magic. So magical that people might think it is luck. But without preparation, there are missed opportunities and missed magical moments.

Women need to not only silence that inner critic but also be intentional about how they uplift others. I have been fortunate to have mentors and friends who call me out when I minimize myself. "You are a CEO," they remind me. "You are making a difference." That is the kind of leadership we must model for ourselves, and for those who are watching and learning from our example. Ask yourself – how are you showing up for others? Do you call women into conversations when they are "*just*-ing" themselves or minimizing their accomplishments? Do you acknowledge the skills and abilities they are bringing to the table?

Recently, on a call with a colleague, she shared the way she acknowledges others' gifts. She observes how they lead and then takes the opportunity to share her observations of their strengths with them. She said it is more than sharing a compliment on a woman's outfit or lipstick color. It's an opportunity for her to share how she sees them showing up and showing out.

Leadership can be lonely, especially if you're one of the few women at the table. Friends, confidantes, and peer groups matter for reducing stress and creating safe spaces. McKinsey & Company's

"Women in the Workplace" report highlights how formal and informal networks—like ERGs (employee resource groups) and peer circles—help women stay in leadership pipelines, negotiate more effectively, and feel greater empowerment. Harvard Business Review confirms "relationship capital" fosters growth, combats anxiety, and counters gender bias.

My own story? My network pushed me to pursue an MBA and HR certifications, opening doors I never knew existed. The Callen Crew? They wore out two pairs of tennis shoes campaigning by my side. The Hibiscus women? They rallied around me during a disruptive career transition, showing up and reminding me that my value and my worth aren't tied to a role. My family? They are my strength. Even when I stumble, they lift me with love and remind me how proud they are – often before I remember to be proud of myself.

Who is your crew, your network, your support system? When you intentionally cultivate strong support systems, friends, peers, mentors, and sponsors, you amplify your capacity. Women who build support systems take more risks, negotiate harder, and step closer to the spotlight. Find your people and invest in those relationships.

I am asking women to become more aware of how, when, and why they *"just"* themselves. Start a log and for a week write down each time you say *"just"* in a way that diminishes you or your value. Begin by checking your emails. A fellow female entrepreneur shared with me that she has removed *"just* checking in" from her email subject line and is now "checking in" with her clients instead. Checking in with folks takes time and energy and has an impact on others. Don't diminish the value of connecting. If you struggle with emails, you can use a Chrome extension – *Just Not Sorry.* This extension warns you when you use words or phrases that can undermine your message. It underlines commonly used qualifying words – I'm sorry, I think, *just*, etc. – and gives you options to modify your sentence. As you keep this log, you may be surprised at how many times you *just* diminish your value without realizing it.

I know I have a mission: I am called to restrict *just* from my vocabulary and to help others do the same. There is no such thing as "I'm *just*."

Take a moment and say this phrase aloud: "I'm *just* a leader."

Now say this phrase: "I *am* a leader."

Do you feel the difference? There is power in removing *just* and in not using the contraction. You're not *just* a leader. You *are* a leader. You're not *just* an advocate. You *are* an advocate. You're not *just* a woman with a voice. You *are* a woman whose voice can change the world.

Earlier you stood up and shouted, with your arms in the air, "You've got this!" I would ask you to now rise to your feet, with one hand on your hip and your other arm in the air, with your hand in a fist. Now state emphatically – "I *am*," and you can choose the descriptor for who you are. If you need some inspiration to get started, perhaps start with one of these: I *am* phenomenal. I *am* a leader. I *am* a role model. I *am* a difference maker. I *am* a change agent.

Do you remember that framed silhouette that Patty gave me for my birthday? I didn't hang that picture on my wall for nearly three months because I *just* struggled with adding myself to this wall of women who changed the world. But in the end, I did, because I know I *am* a bad ass, also. Period.

You have been given the challenge; remove *just* from your vocabulary. Replace hesitation with confidence. Stand in your power. Now more than ever, the world doesn't need women who are "*just*" anything. We need women who know their worth. Women who lead unapologetically. Women who stand up and boldly proclaim, "I *am!*"

CHAPTER 5

Choose to Lead with Love

Gretchen Schott

Growth Strategist, Leadership Coach,
Keynote Speaker, Facilitator

gretchenschott.com

linkedin.com/in/gretchenschott

instagram.com/leadingwell_inspirations

Gretchen Schott is a growth strategist, leadership expert, executive coach, and keynote speaker dedicated to helping individuals and organizations develop strong, effective leaders. She specializes in strategies for coaching, leadership development, team building, change management, and employee engagement, which enable people with the skills to lead to do so with confidence, build trust, and drive meaningful impact.

As the founder of *Leading Well*, she delivers transformative coaching, workshops, and keynotes for leaders seeking to elevate their impact. With over 30 years of experience in leadership, management, and talent development, she has worked in roles that span multiple industries, including technology, financial services, and retail. She is also the Chief Learning Officer at *Threefold*, leading GrowU, by equipping leaders for the next stage of business and fostering a culture of growth and development rooted in accountability, continuous learning and purposeful leadership.

A dynamic speaker and facilitator, Gretchen hosts the podcast *Made for Impact,* offering insights on leadership, growth, and engagement.

Outside of her professional pursuits, Gretchen is an active member of *St. Louis de Montfort* Catholic Church, serving in marriage enrichment and liturgical ministries. She also volunteers and serves at local theatres and productions, fueling her passion for the performing arts.

On January 2nd, 2025, my father took his own life. It was violent and unexpected. I spent many days sitting in my family room, with the fireplace on, staring at my Christmas tree, quietly processing what had happened. I didn't want his life to be defined by his suicide, but rather by the life he had led and the love he had for me and my family. My love of leadership came from him. From a young age, he was pushing Dale Carnegie cassette tapes on me or sending me conference brochures. He taught me I could be a woman leader and to use my femininity to my advantage. He influenced how I lead today.

As I was processing my grief, my family and I were loved so well in the days and weeks that followed. People brought us food, books, and prayers. Some people came and sat with me. Some people sent me text messages, simply saying:

I love you.

You are strong.

You got this.

Each of these loving moments helped me to shine a little brighter and appreciate what it means to be loved well. Maybe you have had a similar experience. Receiving deep love at a time when you needed it most.

When I returned home from my father's funeral, I had to process the loss, and my reaction to it: What is going to bring me joy right now? To be completely honest, I considered bowing out of this opportunity to write with these other authors. I wasn't sure I had the capacity to do this. Many days, I felt like I had a damper over my personal light, and it felt exhausting to work, and joy at work impossible to grasp. But I knew that joy wasn't something to be found—it was something to be created.

I'm a woman that loves creating. I knew when I said "yes" to writing this book, I wanted to learn and enjoy the publishing process. And the more I thought about what brings me joy, the more I felt nudged to continue on this path and commit to achieving this personal goal to become a published author. Through journaling and reflection, I realized, for me, joy at work is leadership. Joy is cultivated when three things are present:

Leading. Learning. Loving.

When all of those are present, I am my best self. And so, I made the choice to continue to lead, to learn, and to love this time in my life. I recommitted to be a part of this anthology in the hopes that I can bring joy to others.

I'm sharing my thoughts on leadership and why we need more leaders choosing to lead with love. As you continue to read, I encourage you to take time to consider:

- What brings you joy?
- What brings you joy at work?
- What defines your leadership?
- What choices can you make to bring more joy into your life and your leadership?

JOY IS A CHOICE

A few months ago, during my prayer time, I stumbled into a disruptive thought. I was listening to a devotional and the host said something about being content.

Now, when you read that, did you read "content" as:

Material dealt with in a speech, literary work, information made available by a website or other electronic medium.

or

A state of happiness and satisfaction.

I started thinking about what it means to feel content. I started reflecting: "When was the last time I felt content?" When I wrote the word *content* down, I realized the word content also means **content,** as pertains to information and data. (*I literally asked Siri to tell me how to spell it because I doubted that I was spelling and using the word properly.*)

In my work as a facilitator, trainer, and coach, I produce and design a lot of content. Creating PowerPoints and learning materials, producing podcast episodes, teaching. . . all of these mediums require me to produce content.

Thinking about content. . . I had to ask myself. . .

Is the content I am consuming bringing me content(ment)?

And. . .

Is the content I am producing helping others consume content that brings them closer to feeling content(ment)?

Creating good content requires a level of vulnerability. Sharing ideas and receiving feedback can be rewarding, but at times, it can also feel uncomfortable. For me, when I am uncomfortable, I know I am growing.

How do you define contentment and joy? I'm a creator, and so, I describe contentment and joy as:

- Contentment – a state of happiness and satisfaction.
- Joy – a feeling of great pleasure and happiness.

You may not realize this, but you choose to work. You choose to be joyful. You also can choose to be miserable. Choosing to be miserable is tormenting. Torment is suffering that lacks clarity or meaning; it's a feeling of being stuck in pain with no way forward.

Maybe you've felt pain at work. Do you connect with any of these statements:

- Staying in a job because you were scared you wouldn't make the same amount of money someplace else.
- Putting up with disrespectful behavior from peers and bosses.
- Tolerating being passed over.
- Making yourself feel guilty for wanting to be recognized, included, asked, or acknowledged for your knowledge, skills, and expertise.

Maybe you can relate. Maybe you're now realizing your discontent at work is making you miserable and you want to stop tormenting yourself (and others around you).

The good news is you can *choose* joy. You choose joy when you know yourself enough to recognize what brings *you* contentment. Contentment leads to joy, and joy is a choice.

Joy at work is not about being happy every moment of the day. It's about identifying moments of gratitude that allow you to affirm your self-worth and confidence. Maybe you're fortunate to have had a job where you experienced incredible joy.

For me, that looked like working for an exciting company where going into the office and seeing my peers brought me happiness. It included loving our company mission and, when I worked late or over the weekends, the time spent in office didn't feel like a sacrifice because I was so invested in what we were doing, and I valued the people around me.

Then this joy-filled company was acquired and became an even bigger and more profitable company. Yet, as the acquisition moved towards merging our two companies, I felt more miserable every day. Can you relate?

The work I loved doing was being decimated. In one meeting with the HR transition team, the business partner turned to me and said, "This work you do over here, developing leaders, we do that for you, so you won't be doing that anymore. And this work aligning customer satisfaction to employee satisfaction, we don't do that and will be eliminating these projects. So. . . now all we need to do is figure out what we want to do with you."

This was said to me in the brightest, perkiest, "we are in this together" tone you can imagine.

I sat there, flabbergasted, and thought, *Well, what I want to do is what I was doing, and it was generating results and retaining our staff.* Shortly after that conversation, I was put through several internal interviews to try and "find a place for me."

This process was humiliating. I shared with the team that I didn't want to relocate and that I didn't want to take a step backward in my career. In response to that, they sent me to an interview out of state at the headquarters and asked me to present a workshop to a small group of people who were so busy putting out customer issues, they didn't even make eye contact or look at me the entire time. Picture walking into an audition and the director simply says, "Your name is. . ." and when you finish singing your heart out, they merely say, "Thank you." and you are escorted out. That is what it felt like.

Shortly after that interview, I was offered a role that would require me to move out of state and take a smaller management role. I knew then, I had all the affirmation I needed to feel confident in my decision to look outside the organization for a new role.

To do that, I had to seek out moments of contentment at work. I declined that role and responded with, "Thank you for the offer, but I am not interested. What else can we explore?"

I transitioned to a role where my expertise was valued, allowing me to succeed as a project manager. This gave me the time to search for a job that would bring me joy again.

Joy at work is a choice. How can you prepare yourself for finding contentment and joy?

Decide right now that you want to experience great pleasure and happiness in your work. Dismiss the fears, the "what ifs," and the "I don't know how's" and instead identify what brings *you* personal joy.

As an executive coach, I often find it helpful to provide my clients with an exercise to help them identify and move past beliefs and thoughts that are preventing them from experiencing true joy at work. I call this exercise, "The Highlight Reel." In it, you identify moments of deep satisfaction and fulfillment throughout your life and career. It's helpful to come up with three to five moments you felt the most accomplished and happiest. Then ask yourself, *what was I doing? Who was I working with? What impact did it have? Why did it matter to me?*

LEADERSHIP IS A CHOICE

Leadership, like joy, is a choice. Leadership is different from management. A disruptive and compelling article that shaped my beliefs is "Moving from Individual to Relationship: A Postindustrial Paradigm of Leadership" by Joseph C. Rost, from the *Journal of Leadership & Organizational Studies.* In his work, Rost makes the bold claim that "leadership is an influence relationship and management is an authority relationship." This view changed how I lead, promote leadership, and attract leaders, as well as demonstrated how to engage and retain key talent across an organization.

If you are like me, much of what I was taught about leadership focused on management. Specifically, concepts around how to manage people through a set of goals and tasks, how to manage and resolve conflicts, and how to perform effective performance reviews. The idea that *influence* is leadership and authority is management simply blew my mind.

Reflecting on your own leadership journey, when have you demonstrated strong influence versus strong management? There have absolutely been times in my career when I didn't have a team of direct reports but I had a strong influence, which produced results. There have also been times when I was managing teams of people, using influence to accomplish goals and outcomes.

If you are a leader, you *may* also be a manager, but you *don't have to be a manager* to be considered a leader in your organization. Leaders exhibit influence. They can win others over, practice strong communication, and desire to achieve success and enable the success of others. Managers give direction, inform subordinates, and often ensure their success through their ability to manage tasks.

You need to choose *leadership*, and you do that when you embrace humility, motivation, and confidence. When you have all three, you are embracing personal growth. Personal growth leads to engagement. Engagement leads to making an impact on the world.

I had the false belief for many years that, to be a good leader and make an impact, I had to always be available. All the people pleasers out there know what I mean. One of my favorite words is "yes!" I still struggle with wanting to do so much and never feeling like I have enough time to get everything done. I remember thinking (and probably was advised poorly) that "If I'm always available and always willing, I'll be rewarded." I valued being favored, or hopefully promoted, over others, which led to me often feeling discouraged, resentful, and burned out. When I made the decision to stop striving for the next promotion in my company and choose to focus on being my best self, I became a lot more joyful at work.

The area where I often slip up is overcommitting time and underestimating interest and ability. How you choose to spend your time is also a choice. Have your choices created less joy and more stress?

An exercise I give my clients is to "Clean the Windshield." Have you ever been in your car and your windshield is a little smudged? You can see out the windshield and drive, but it's not as clear or sharp as it would be if the windshield was cleaned. You turn on the wipers and *swipe* – now you can drive more confidently and clearly. You can do this same thing when you want to get a clearer picture of your leadership and resolve conflicts. You have the answers within you about what to do, and what needs to get done.

For a more detailed explanation, including a downloadable version of this exercise, visit my resources page: www.gretchenschott.com/resources.

Leadership is a choice. You can choose to be clear, focused, and intentional, or you can choose to be stressed, frantic, and chaotic. You choose how you lead, and the best leaders lead with love.

LEADING WITH LOVE IS A CHOICE

"Joy is the simplest form of gratitude."
– Saint Pope John Paul II

If joy is a choice, and leadership is a choice, then *how* you lead is also a choice. Leading with love is when you lead with humility, choosing to value others and to be grateful for the opportunity to serve others.

Each year, I identify one word to be my life's annual theme. I have adopted this practice for over ten years, and many of my friends and colleagues join me in doing this. To make this practice "stick" and not just fluff, I intentionally select a Scripture verse that embodies what I hope to reveal in myself by the end of the year. I create a Pinterest board and collect articles and images that are representative of that word. I share my word with others for accountability.

The hardest word I chose a few years ago was "humility." Sharing with people that you are working on being humble is an invitation for people to let you know when you are *not* being humble. That year I was introduced to a prayer called the *Litany of Humility*, written by Rafael Cardinal Merry del Val y Zulueta. This prayer was life-changing for me and continues to fill me spiritually as I do the hard work to grow personally. Most everything in the prayer are things I desire and want for myself.

I realized I wanted those things by forsaking others. Focusing on **myself** and **my** success over others instead of succeeding **with** others. Recognizing this changed my life. I grew in showing and having gratitude towards others. Personal strengths and gifts were clear when I was serving others, as opposed to serving myself. Fortunately, I was working with a team of people who believed in growth and valued personal development.

At work, personal engagement is increased when the work environment or company allows you to be humble, motivated, and confident. I define these values in this way:

- Humility – valuing others as much or more than ourselves.
- Motivation – possessing the desire to be successful with and for the benefit of others.
- Confidence – believing that you can trust yourself and your abilities, and that you have a sense of control in your life.

I've shared how I came to practice and understand a deeper sense of humility in my life and being a humble and loving leader. Understanding what is personally motivating for you can also be instrumental in leading with love. Personal motivation may show up as:

- Showing enthusiasm and excitement for your work
- Taking ownership for your responsibilities
- Supporting others
- Learning and self-improvement

If you are leading with humility, motivation, and confidence, you are leading with love. It may sound "fluffy" or "soft" to say "I choose to lead with love," but the reality is, you likely already are and simply don't recognize it. You may have experienced managers who have led you, being loving, and didn't call it "leading with love." Here are some examples of what leading with love looks like:

- When you choose to be an ally for someone who doesn't feel confident or empowered to speak up. . . You are leading with love.

- When you call out coworkers for making inappropriate jokes and remarks that make you uncomfortable and make them look bad. . . You are leading with love.

- When an employee comes into your office and tells us they are ill and is crying and you offer a box of tissues and ask more questions. . . You are leading with love.

- When you listen to an employee who is just miserable at work and can't see themselves being successful. . . and you help them to accept they need to find a new job elsewhere. . . You are leading with love.

I want to encourage you to choose to lead with love and create joy at work for yourself and others. You can't lead others until you know yourself. You can't create joy at work if you don't know what joy is for you.

Leadership focused on joy and love requires clarity of your own self-worth. In Jamie Kern Lima's book, *Worthy*, she eloquently defined the difference between self-worth and self-confidence. She defined self-worth as the internal, deep-rooted belief that you are enough and worthy of love and belonging, just as you are, and self-confidence as an assessment of how you compare and evaluate yourself based on your qualities, skills, and traits.

As leaders, self-confidence is helpful, and developing confidence and competence are crucial for personal success, but knowing your self-worth is foundational for becoming the leader you desire to be. It is also grounded in humility, motivation, and confidence.

To strengthen your sense of self-worth, try this exercise. Recall a time you felt happy and proud—focus on that feeling. List your wins from the past nine months (health, relationships, finances, spirituality, work). Ask yourself, *What will success look like by year-end?* and *I'll know I've achieved it because. . .* Describe how you want to feel and who you'll celebrate with. Choose one action this week to take that will move you toward that vision. Finally, close your eyes, take three deep breaths, and picture your success.

Can you imagine how much more productive and fulfilled you would be if, as a leader, you paused and asked yourself, "How can I behave in a more loving manner in this situation?" or "How can I best show this person I see them and hear them?"

Do something for me. Put down the book and pull out your phone. Send a text to someone important to you. Text them "You. Love. Me. Well." and hit send. This small acknowledgement of love will change your relationship with this person for the better. When you receive texts back from these important people in your life, share with them one specific thing they do for you that lets you know you are loved well.

I would love to hear how your relationships improve and how this small step led to something new for you! If you're ready to grow, I'd be honored to work with you. You can learn more about the coaching I offer at www.gretchenschott.com/contact and select the option for "Intentional Leadership Coaching Engagement." You can share your own stories with me here as well, if you select "Share Your *Joy@Work* Story."

I hope you've been inspired to think and act differently, and that you accept my invitation to lead with love and **love well**. The world needs better leaders. **You can choose to be one of them.**

CHAPTER 6

Joyful Resilience: A Productive Response to Life

Sarah Turner

Leadership Consultant, Speaker, and Coach

luminoleadership.com

linkedin.com/in/sarahgturner

luminoleadership.com/joyful-resilience-resources

As founder and president of Lumino Leadership, Sarah serves as a professional trainer, consultant, and executive coach. Her specialties include customized training programs for developing strong leaders, personalized coaching plans to assist in determining and achieving goals, and customized support for corporate initiatives to maximize success. She has multiple certifications, including the Emotional Intelligence instruments EQ-i 2.0® and EQ 360®, and the HRG (Hardiness Resilience Gauge), as well as DISC, Platinum Rule™, and the Predictive Index™. She is also a certified Corporate Athlete®.

With a strong business background in public accounting and years spent working in corporate talent development, Sarah brings a unique perspective to all levels of employees in a variety of industries. Her passion for helping individuals grow as a way to capitalize on an organization's most precious resource, its people, creates a dynamic, powerful formula for results.

In addition, she is actively involved in developing the young leaders of tomorrow, serving on the board of directors of the nationally acclaimed Hugh O'Brian Youth Leadership Program for her home state of Indiana.

W hen you think of the hard times in your life, do you recall feeling joy? Most of us are far more likely to recall feeling fear, anxiety, frustration, or anger. In fact, if I asked you to list your most commonly used words to describe difficult situations, I am guessing the word "joy" would not even make your list. And yet, joy can be present if we know how to harness the power of resilience to make use of adversity properly.

My mom was one of nine kids growing up in a single-income home with 11 mouths to feed. Grandpa was a hard-working dad who gave everything he had to ensure his family had their basic needs met and more love than they could ever need. Grandma stayed home with my aunts and uncle and was an exceptional problem-solver. She never wasted anything and could repurpose the most random things in her house to solve whatever challenges life brought her way. I remember watching her take plastic bags to crochet them into rugs for the house when I was a kid. She was amazing! As my mom grew up, she saw my Grandma's ability to resiliently respond to the circumstances presented to her firsthand and absorbed that talent herself, which, in turn, impacted the trajectory of my life as well.

In the mid-1980s, as a young girl, my parents allowed us to watch a few TV shows. One of my favorites was MacGyver. I never got tired of watching the lead character create a solution out of whatever random resources he had at the time. When he built a telescope using a magnifying glass, a watch crystal, and some newspaper, you couldn't help but be impressed with his ingenuity. Growing up, I always thought my mom was the OG MacGyver! There was no problem she couldn't solve with the barest resources and/or supply of whatever we had lying around the house.

Dozens of times my sister, brother, or I would throw something at her last minute, such as, "Mom, I forgot I need a costume for a skit we are doing for English tomorrow."

Her response would be to pause, ask what it had to look like, and immediately start walking around our house, looking in every closet, collecting random things: a glue gun, a swath of fabric, a piece of foil, an unmatched sock, and maybe get out the sewing machine, just in case. She would spend twenty minutes be-bopping around, often humming a tune, occasionally holding up her masterpiece in the making until she would present to you her solution to the last-minute request. It may not have been purchased from a professional store, but it always met the criteria and was made in the calmest way.

She never got rattled, blamed us for causing her undue stress, or appeared ill-prepared to accomplish the task. In fact, her mindset carried a sense of *joy* to be able to help us in our moment of panic. Because of her consistent, productive response to unplanned challenges, I got to witness the pure power of resilience and learn how to positively respond to stress.

> Hardiness represents a pattern of behavior we can choose as responders to the adverse conditions that creep into our lives.

As a leadership consultant, I have spent nearly two decades intrigued by the concept of how we respond to the triggers in our lives. There are so many different types of activating events and, whether we like it or not, how we choose to react in each setting determines the types of outcomes we experience. Now, if you are like me, you wonder, *is there anything I can do about it?* The good news is, there is!

Dr. Paul T. Bartone, a research psychologist in the U.S. Army, and Dr. Steven J. Stein discovered through a study that resilience is made up of lots of factors, but the biggest piece of the pie is our level of "hardiness." In their book, *Hardiness: Making Stress Work for You to Achieve Your Life Goal,* they share a model that has made a significant difference in how I respond to the elements of stress in my life, and I am fortunate to see its positive impact in the lives of those I coach.

Let me first share that, as I was becoming familiar with the term "hardiness," I kept defaulting to being a young kid, playing in my yard as my dad walked around looking for weeds. We had a small yard, but my dad was keen on making sure it was well taken care of and often could be seen walking back and forth with a bottle of weed killer, ready to aim it at whatever weed was making its way back up into our lawn. His usage of the word "hardy" to describe our weeds created an association, in my mind, with the pesky things that kept him on high alert, like a watchdog ready to pounce!

While that is not likely what Dr. Bartone and Dr. Stein intended to represent the term, I quickly realized the association is actually quite accurate in demonstrating what the concept references in our human behavior. Hardiness represents a pattern of behavior we can choose as responders to the adverse conditions that creep into our lives. We can build our level of hardiness and deal with fatigue or hardships in such a way that we create desired outcomes both personally and professionally.

The modeled path for how to grow hardiness is a powerful three-part framework (illustrated below), with each element measured in low, moderate, or high usage. All three are capable of being developed through intentional action to build new response habits.

CHALLENGE

Seeing change and novelty as exciting and as an opportunity for you to learn and grow

CONTROL

Having a sense of self-efficacy and the belief that you can influence outcomes in your life

COMMITMENT

Being engaged and seeing most parts of your life as interesting and meaningful

HOW TO POSITION YOUR LEVEL OF CHALLENGE

Of all three categories of hardiness, "challenge" is the one I see my clients work hardest to keep in shape and ready for use. By definition, this factor measures our propensity to see change as an opportunity for growth.

Like most humans, I can get apprehensive about new things. I especially worry about the things my kids are facing today that I did not face growing up, and hope I can help them think of new, innovative ways to solve problems, as opposed to always defaulting to handling them the way I did "when I was your age." Novel things can be exciting, but they can also be hard to face head-on, and this hardiness factor requires us to see through a unique lens when looking at stress.

I'm a huge fan of Kelly McGonigal's research on the way we look at stress. In her book, *The Upside of Stress*, she shares two different views we can carry regarding stress. The first is that stress is harmful to us. This is called the *threat response*. The second is that stress can be good for us. This is called the *challenge response*. If you pause for a moment and consider your perspective today, ask yourself the question: Do you think stress is good or bad for you? What would you say and what is your answer based upon?

As a keynote speaker who commonly gets to share my love of the topic of resilience, I have asked thousands of people this question. By far, the vast majority will say, "It's bad for you." We traditionally carry a negative sentiment about what stress does to us. We have all been personally affected or seen loved ones impacted by the power of stress on our physical health. Whether it be small-scale symptoms, such as nausea or headaches, or large-scale symptoms, such as high blood pressure or even heart attacks, the history of seeing example after example of unwanted predicaments leads us to believe we don't want stress in our lives. While no one hopes to increase physical ailments, the fact is, we have also all had moments when stress was the catalyst for a higher quality version of ourselves to show up and create value.

Consider your time as a student, when you procrastinated studying for an exam. Many times, as anxiety started to soar, we used the stress to dial up our focus and amplify our learning capacity to do well on the test. When you competed in a sport, remember a time when your adrenaline spiked and you channeled the extra energy into running faster, jumping further, or aiming truer for the desired goal for the event. The reality is every situation that includes stress can be looked at as unwanted trouble or as a partner for success. The most refreshing thing about that statement is the word "can," because it means we can choose.

GUIDANCE ON GROWING YOUR LEVEL OF CHALLENGE:

When exploring the hardiness factor of *challenge*, how we develop is linked to our mindset towards the situations we face. The goal is to train our minds to see moments of change, or new or unclear settings, as an opportunity for value in our lives. To do this, we must direct our mental energy towards developing new habits and increasing our comfort with unfamiliar or undesirable predicaments. To get you thinking about how to begin, here are some of my favorite suggestions for those I coach:

1. **Find your next challenge.** Determine a reasonable cadence for trying things outside your comfort zone. Ask those with skills or characteristics you desire about their journey. As you get started, this could include little things like trying a food you have never had, reading a book you wouldn't normally open, or creating a long-term commitment to try something new each week for a year.

2. **Commit and compete with yourself first.** Plan when and how you will engage in a new activity and give the task a home on your calendar. Once you start, try to avoid using others (especially those seasoned at a skill/activity) as your mark of success. Consider the level of your skills or performance before you begin and build from there.

3. **Use your history as fuel.** Make a list of past behaviors and accomplishments. What is your history when it comes to learning new things, and what examples do you have where you successfully improved a skill in your life? Once you reflect, create a plan to repeat your success habits in future moments of stress and adversity to "challenge" the moment and bounce back with some of your most trusted skills.

4. **Embrace failure.** Learn how to celebrate mistakes. Consider exploring the concept of *grit* (Angela Duckworth's book is a great start) as you develop habits to unpack a moment of failure and use it as a catalyst for growth.

HOW TO POSITION YOUR LEVEL OF CONTROL

Of all the hardiness categories, this is the one senior leaders ask me about the most, based on the significant potential it has on the value within a company. Using empowerment properly is an invaluable characteristic that helps organizations push through tough, often unexpected moments, but it hinges on the amount of ownership and control applied by the empowered party.

The core element to measuring this factor is possessing the belief we can influence the situations in our lives. Just like all three hardiness categories, we can be anywhere from low to high in this space. When you are low, you want to throw your hands up and say things like: "It's not like I can make a difference" or "That's above my pay grade." You simply don't see a path where your efforts could help steer the outcome. However, when you are at a high level in this space, you carry a strong belief in your efforts and are willing to make choices and take responsibility for your actions even amidst stress or change.

While our roles often have a direct impact on our level of authority, having a low level of this hardiness factor can have a significant impact on results. No matter our title, our willingness to try to contribute to solving problems can make the difference between quickly making decisions and timely pivoting or sitting idle, waiting for others to take the lead, losing precious time along the way. Leaders recognize this characteristic as a needed skill set and, similar to all hardiness categories, we can expand our level of *control* with intentional targets for growth.

GUIDANCE ON GROWING YOUR LEVEL OF CONTROL:

In all facets of my life, I have to flex my "control muscles" of *hardiness*, but, as a mom of two teenage boys, I find this one on constant standby to get me through the day! Some of my favorite activities to expand this area of resilience include:

1. **Using your mental energy wisely.** Wasting brain power ruminating about things that you shouldn't control drains mental energy, leaving less power for creative endeavors. Focus on things that will make the most difference when deciding where to influence situations toward a productive end.

My example of late is the "hair battle" with my sons. Since I don't quite understand the newest trend of wanting your hair to look intentionally messy, I spent months arguing with my boys, trying to get them to change their hairstyle before leaving the house. Over time, I realized I was creating undue stress in an area that was not the most important factor for me to control. It helps to know what to let go of and when to direct that same energy into places that will benefit greatly from your contributions.

2. **Developing coping mechanisms.** Stress tolerance is a valuable emotional intelligence skill that can increase your hardiness factor of *control*. Using coping strategies like counting down from 100 by intervals of three, square breathing, or even going for a walk when you feel control slipping can help you get back to neutral and provide clarity in the moment to plan your actions wisely.

3. **Breaking tasks down into manageable chunks.** This is a commonly used tactic and can be highly effective at increasing the feasibility of control. Be realistic as you position time and resources for each "chunk" of work.

4. **Creating healthy boundaries.** Setting up guardrails is an exceptional tool for growth. As an example, if you know you often jump to conclusions during challenging moments, increase control of your responses by setting a new boundary whereby you cannot share your opinion without pausing to ask a question to learn more first. Over time, this will become a habit, naturally increasing your control and hardiness during times of adversity.

HOW TO POSITION YOUR LEVEL OF COMMITMENT

In looking at the three areas of hardiness we can use to redesign our responses to adversity, building your level of *commitment*, in my opinion, is the most powerful. In a manner of speaking, I see this factor as the amplifier of resilience and have witnessed its impact on the other two hardiness categories firsthand.

By definition, this factor measures our alignment to meaning in all aspects of our lives and helps steer our response by elevating our will to strategically react to accomplish our most important objectives.

Consider the number of things you spend time on in your life. What percentage are so important, you would not be persuaded to divert attention from them, as opposed to the percentage you would gladly give up because you do not see how they relate to your work or your life? The data collected in answering this question is tied to your hardiness level of commitment.

When we don't care about something and a moment of adversity arises, we are likely to say, "I don't even know what we are doing here. Maybe we should bail on this approach and start over." We, in turn, don't lean into the *challenge* presented to us and pull back on our level of *control*, primarily because we don't care enough to lean into the moment fully. On the other hand, when we really care about something and an unexpected curve ball gets thrown our way, we are likely to say, "Okay. That was not planned, but this presents us with an opportunity to unpack the situation, learn what caused it, and redirect our efforts in a more productive way to stay on track to get our targeted results." We mentally, emotionally, and physically embrace the *challenge* and increase our influence via our *control* to ensure we get to the destination we imagined.

GUIDANCE ON GROWING YOUR LEVEL OF COMMITMENT:

This area requires a deeper look at yourself and, for that reason, is often least prioritized for growth. While the journey may, at times, push you out of your comfort zone, the rewards are well worth the effort. Some key activities to grow this area of resilience include:

1. **Defining what matters most.** Intentionally making a list of the things you want to accomplish (both personally and professionally) is a key starting point for developing *commitment*. By creating a personal mission statement or a targeted list of desired outcomes for your life, you can readily decide where to spend your time and energy.

2. **Establishing a support system to keep yourself accountable.** Once you determine what matters most, having observers willing to keep you aligned is invaluable. Give them permission to ask how you are doing on a commitment in your life and allow them to help you get back on track, as needed.

3. **Saying "no" when needed or finding out the "why."** Too often, we feel obligated to say "yes" to things that we do not feel connected to simply to be compliant or less disruptive. Unknowingly, we slide our level of *commitment* down, which often makes us less willing to accept *challenges* or increase our *control* to ensure success. In that case, your ability to say "no" or "help me understand the *why* behind this request" can be a critical step in redirecting time, energy, and resources properly for all involved.

4. **Practicing gratitude.** This is one of the best ways to increase commitment. Start using a gratitude journal (or you can list the relevant things aloud to yourself) and challenge yourself to reflect on the elements you feel thankful for. This sense of gratefulness acts as fuel to ensure we re-prioritize future experiences to increase resilience and create value for ourselves and others.

FINAL THOUGHTS

Since becoming a certified hardiness coach more than five years ago, I have been fortunate to witness growth in both myself and those I coach. The stories of resilience, of people pushing their *challenge* mindset while applying higher levels of *control*, fueled by their *commitment* to create value, are a constant inspiration for me to continue growing my hardiness and share its untapped value with others. My resounding thoughts are that stress and adversity don't have to equate to negative moments. On the contrary, they can produce powerful moments of joy and engagement repeatedly, with a little intentionality. My hope is that this conversation spurs interest within you to explore the concept further and try activities for positioning hardiness to positively impact your life.

Fortunately, for me, my mom was an amazing example of high application of all three categories of hardiness. She embraced new things, calmly called upon skills she had built from past moments, examined her results based on her own capabilities first, didn't mind failing as long as she learned something to put in her tool kit for future moments, and applied her influence in ideal places based on her unwavering sense of purpose and values. Her status as the OG MacGyver was the penultimate mentoring experience, and I will endeavor to do the same for others as often as possible!

If you are intrigued and would like to know more, let's connect! I have more resources located at www.luminoleadership.com/joyful-resilience-resources. I would welcome the chance to hear about your experiences on your journey to gather joy through expanding your hardiness!

Conclusion

*J*oy@Work: When Women Lead is more than a collection of stories—it's a movement. Through courage, vulnerability, insight, and wisdom, each author in this anthology has illuminated the many paths to leadership. These are grounded not in hierarchy or perfection, but in purpose, self-awareness, and joy.

"Superpowers!" is a reminder that joy begins with knowing and owning our unique strengths. I invite us all to discover our inner brilliance and use it as fuel for leadership that uplifts ourselves and others.

Jill Lehman's chapter, "You-Powered: Charting the Course to Career Joy," provides a roadmap for reclaiming agency in our professional lives. Her voice encourages intentional career ownership, reminding us that fulfillment comes not from luck but from bold, consistent choices rooted in self-awareness.

In "All's Well That Ends," Kerrie Weinzapfel guides us through the inevitable transitions of a career with grace and perspective. She offers a profound truth: even in endings, joy can be found, if we are willing to look for it and lead ourselves through with hope and reflection.

MeChelle Callen uses "Just" to shine a light on the subtle but powerful ways language can diminish or elevate. Her bold call to stop minimizing ourselves with words like "just" is both a challenge and a rallying cry for every woman to take up space, claim her worth, and lead unapologetically.

Gretchen Schott's "Choose to Lead with Love" reminds us that love is not a soft skill, it's a revolutionary one. Her chapter shows how heart-centered leadership creates cultures where people thrive, and how choosing love is an act of both courage and strength.

Finally, Sarah Turner's "Joyful Resilience: A Productive Response to Life" reframes resilience as more than endurance: it is an intentional, empowering mindset. She shows us how we can cultivate hardiness in ourselves and others by choosing joy even in the face of adversity.

Together, these voices form a chorus that echoes a powerful truth: When women lead with authenticity, strength, and joy, they don't just change their own lives—they change the world around them. This anthology is both a mirror and a map for every reader ready to lead from within, to choose joy, and to power their work with purpose.

The journey doesn't end here. Let this be the beginning of your own Joy@Work story.

• • •

Will You Share the Love?

If you've enjoyed *Joy@Work*, the authors have a favor to ask.

Would you consider giving it a rating wherever you bought the book? Online book stores are more likely to promote a book when they feel good about its content, and reader reviews are a great barometer for a book's quality.

Also, if you have found this book valuable and know others who would find it useful, consider buying them a copy as a gift. Special bulk discounts are available if you would like your whole team or organization to benefit from reading this. Just contact jodee@purpleinkllc.com or visit getjoypowered.com.

• • •

Bring the Power of Joy@Work to Your Organization

If you're inspired by the powerful insights in *Joy@Work: When Women Lead*, imagine the impact these authors could have speaking directly to your team or coaching within your organization. Each woman brings a unique voice and proven leadership experience. Reach out to any of the authors to explore keynotes, workshops, or coaching engagements—and bring more joy, purpose, and power to your workplace.

• • •

Have an Idea for Your Own Anthology?

If you've enjoyed reading this anthology, imagine the impact of leading your own. Creating an anthology allows you to position yourself as a connector, a leader, and a trusted authority in your field. By inviting your colleagues, clients, or business associates to co-author with you, you give them a powerful platform to share their voice—and you get to shine by association. Everyone benefits from increased visibility, credibility, and the prestige of being a published author. It's also a smart, strategic way to deepen professional relationships and open the door to new opportunities. Whether your network includes coaches, consultants, entrepreneurs, or experts in any field, an anthology gives them a meaningful way to stand out. If this experience inspired you, consider paying it forward—your own anthology might just be the catalyst someone else needs to take their next big step.

If you would like to explore this, reach out to Cathy Fyock at cathy@cathyfyock.com.

Do You Need a Book Coach? Let Me Tell You What I Do!

Do you need a cheerleader? I encourage you when you're feeling defeated or that the task is just too hard.

Do you need a brainstorming partner? We work together to discover a new way to approach your topic.

Do you need a developmental reviewer? My clients are often terrified that they will publish a book—a rather permanent bit of documentation—that is less than excellent. I promise you that I will always provide my candid assessment of your work, so you are free to write (and not focus on editing as you write). I read your book as you write it, and again after your rewrites..

Do you need an accountability partner? If you tell me that you need to get this book completed by year end, I will let you know where you need to be to hit that goal at our weekly meetings.

Do you need a visionary? You may have a limited view of your possibilities. I help you think bigger. I encourage you to reach higher. I'm your possibility partner (which was my original tagline when I began my business 10 years ago).

Do you need writing and publishing resources? While I do developmental editing, I don't copy edit, publish, offer legal advice, and other services that you may need. I know great resources that can meet these needs, and I help you select the best resources.

Do you need a teacher to show you the ropes? I offer classes and education on many aspects of writing, publishing, and book promotion, and where I'm not qualified as a teacher, I position other experts to provide educational events.

Do you need a therapist? I now know that I may need to talk you "off the ledge." Sometimes the authorship journey becomes overwhelming, or the negative voices are too loud, and I stand ready to help you get back at your writing desk.

Do you need a trusted advisor? I will tell it to you straight. I have your back. I'm here for you.

I am The Business Book Strategist and I work with thought leaders and professionals who want to write a nonfiction book about their expertise as a strategy to grow their business, their brand, and their business. Since starting my book coaching business in 2014, I've helped more than 250 professionals become published authors.

If you're interested in scheduling a complimentary strategy session, contact Cathy Fyock at Cathy@CathyFyock.com.

• • •

Other Anthologies Lead by Cathy Fyock

IGNITE
P R E S S ®

You're an Expert.
Does the World Know It?

Ready to transform your expertise into a bestselling book? Ignite Press is your trusted publishing partner, guiding entrepreneurs, professionals, and speakers to achieve #1 bestseller status and elevate their authority.

Led by international bestselling author Everett O'Keefe, Ignite Press offers personalized consultations covering title development, cover design, book creation strategies, and powerful launch campaigns. With over 150 #1 bestsellers and 33 international #1 titles, their track record speaks volumes.

Whether you're a business leader, medical expert, or thought leader, Ignite Press helps you craft a compelling book that amplifies your brand and message. Better yet, you maintain complete ownership of your intellectual property. You also get your books at cost and receive all royalties.

Take the first step—schedule your free consultation today and discover how Ignite Press can turn your story into a powerful tool for influence and growth.

Visit https://IgnitePress.us